Compost

Compost

Essential know-how and expert advice for gardening success

CONTENTS

Compost recycles the nutrients and microorganisms in your kitchen scraps and garden waste, then returns them to the soil, boosting the performance of your ornamental plants and productive crops.

WHY COMPOST?

Making compost at home is an eco-friendly way of using kitchen and plant waste to create what many gardeners refer to as "black gold" because of the wealth of benefits it offers. The main function of compost is to condition the soil, improving drainage on heavy clays while enabling sandy soils to retain more moisture. It also contains essential nutrients and encourages worm activity, helping to increase soil fertility and feed plants slowly as the organic matter breaks down. These rewards are combined with benefits to the wider environment, such as reducing landfill and other forms of pollution.

WHY MAKE COMPOST?

Seasoned gardeners know that if you create a healthy soil, your plants will look after themselves, and nothing does this job better than homemade compost. Although it contains low levels of nutrients compared to many artificial fertilizers, compost delivers its benefits over a long period, which is good for your plants and for the environment. It also conditions the soil, so that it holds water and drains well too. In addition, composting helps to lower your carbon footprint by using free waste materials that you would normally put in the recycling bin or throw away.

Composting at home produces a free soil conditioner and slow-release plant food with a negligible carbon footprint.

Transform your kitchen scraps and garden waste into compost for use on all areas of the garden.

WASTE NOT, WANT NOT

Some local authorities regularly collect garden and kitchen waste, which they process on a large scale to produce compost for the agricultural and landscaping industries and for home gardeners. However, giving away your green waste for others to recycle means that you are losing out on this valuable resource, which is easy to make at home using similar techniques on a smaller scale. Recycling your kitchen and garden waste also saves you the cost of buying soil conditioners and fertilizers, and minimizes your carbon footprint since it requires no transportation or industrial processing. Put simply, it is a win-win option.

THE FREE SOIL CONDITIONER

The compost you make in your garden is an invaluable soil conditioner. It improves the structure of the soil so that it retains more moisture, air, and plant nutrients, while also allowing excess water to drain away, thereby preventing waterlogging. When spread over the surface of clay soils it also stops hard, impermeable crusts from forming, which can cause run-off and flooding during storms. The way in which these ideal soil conditions are created is complex, but in essence it is due to the organic matter, fungi, and bacteria found in compost, which glue together the soil particles so that they are of an optimum size for healthy plant growth (see also pp.12–13). Worms and other minibeasts that live in the soil and feed on compost also play a part in improving its structure and making it more fertile. Their tunnelling creates airways and passageways for water to pass through, while their faeces are rich in plant nutrients.

Compost contains organic matter and microbes that glue soil particles together to create the perfect growing conditions.

Annual applications of compost will enrich the soil with essential nutrients to keep garden and potted plants healthy.

Weeds that germinate in a compost mulch are easy to remove by hand.

NATURAL WEED SUPPRESSANT

Compost is often used to help keep weeds at bay. Applying a thick layer over the soil surface, known as a mulch, excludes light and prevents weed seeds beneath it from germinating. Seeds that fall on to this mulch layer will germinate, but its loose structure makes them easy to pull out or hoe off. In addition, compost aids plant growth, and strong leafy canopies will also restrict weeds by shading the soil and using up the nutrients they need to thrive.

SLOW-RELEASE PLANT FOOD

The plants and green kitchen waste that you add to a compost heap are made up of various chemical elements, such as carbon, nitrogen, phosphorus, and potassium, which are released into the mix during the composting process. When compost is then applied to the soil, these essential nutrients, which sustain growth, flowering, and fruiting, become available for plants to use – and because the decomposition process continues after the compost is in the soil, nutrients are released and delivered to plants over a long period, rather than in one hit, as is the case with most synthetic fertilizers.

Bacteria and fungi are responsible for breaking down the organic matter into its chemical components (see pp.24–25), while another type of fungi known as mycorrhizae, which live on and in roots, help to transfer these nutrients to the plants. The good soil structure created by compost also ensures that the chemicals are not washed away, thereby helping nature to recycle them from one generation of plants to the next.

IT'S EASY!

Busy people may think that making compost will take up too much time and energy. This may be true if you want a fast turnaround – some methods will produce usable compost within two or three months – but there are many techniques to choose from and some require very little effort (see pp.56–65). The compost may take longer to produce, but remember that all organic matter will break down eventually, with no human intervention at all.

WHAT IS COMPOST?

Compost is partially decomposed organic material that can be applied to the soil or used in pots to help plants grow. The term is broadly used to encompass a variety of home-made or commercially available products, and is sometimes confused with "fertilizer", which is different in several key respects (*see pp.88–89*). Compost forms over a long time in a natural environment such as a woodland, where complex compounds that make up dead plants and animals break down into simpler chemicals that plants can use for growth.

Compost can be made in an open heap, but the process is usually faster when organic matter is enclosed in a bin.

Garden and kitchen waste can be recycled in a bin or on a heap, where it will decompose into valuable compost.

NATURAL CYCLES

The elements that make up the bodies of plants and animals are finite, and for life to proceed on Earth they must be continuously recycled from one generation to the next. Key to this is the process of decomposition, which begins as soon as organisms die. Their organic components are consumed by bacteria and fungi as well as by larger creatures, such as worms and beetles, all of which break them up into smaller compounds. These compounds are then absorbed by the roots of living plants, which in turn die or are eaten, so continuing the cycle of life, death, and decomposition.

In a natural environment such as a temperate forest, the recycling of animal and plant material into nutrient-rich organic matter takes several years, but by employing the techniques of composting, we can greatly speed up the process in our gardens. Making compost is a simple way of harnessing the natural processes through which key elements (especially nitrogen and phosphorus, which are essential for plant growth) pass from dead organic matter to living plants.

UNDERSTANDING HUMUS

Compost is composed of organic material that has only partly broken down. Once applied to the soil, it continues to decompose and release nutrients to feed your plants over a long period. When it has given up all of its nutrients, what remains is a carbon-rich, dark brown, spongy, water-retentive material known as "humus". Scientists do not all agree on exactly what humus is, but it is known that it binds tiny clay soil particles together so that they form larger aggregates, which open up voids between them that allow air and water to pass through. In this way, humus helps to increase drainage in clay soils. Humus also coats larger sand particles in free-draining soils, so that they hold on to moisture and trap nutrients, making both available for plants to use (see pp.12–13). Soils with stable structures are protected from erosion too.

Humus is a component of compost and may take centuries to break down.

TYPES OF COMPOST

This book focuses on making your own compost for use in the garden. This dark brown product is intended to be applied to soil to improve its structure, boosting its ability to retain moisture, and acting as a natural slow-release plant food. There are, however, other growing media, also referred to as compost, that have other applications. These products can be bought from your local garden centre – or, with a little knowledge, made more economically in your own garden.

MULTI-PURPOSE COMPOST This is the compost that you'll most often see being sold in large plastic sacks at your

Homemade compost helps retain soil moisture and boosts plant growth.

Potting compost is typically lighter in texture than homemade compost.

garden centre. It is not designed to improve or condition your soil, but to provide a good medium for growing plants in containers. Some formulations of multi-purpose, or potting, compost contain peat, which has been dug from increasingly endangered peat bogs: these composts should be avoided. Other ingredients in multi-purpose composts include coir, coconut husks, bark, woodfibre, and green plant material. Many also contain plant fertilizers. You can make your own eco-friendly potting compost by following the recipes on pp.96–97.

SEED COMPOST Proprietary versions of seed compost contain similar ingredients to multi-purpose compost, as well as vermiculite, a volcanic

Soil-based composts usually contain a high percentage of sterilized loam.

mineral that expands when hydrated, helping to maintain moisture levels. Seed composts contain fewer nutrients than multi-purpose composts, because germination rates are better in less fertile conditions. Rather than buying plastic bags of seed compost, make your own from homemade compost and leafmould.

SOIL-BASED COMPOST This compost is used for plants that will be grown in containers for longer than a year or two. It may contain peat (check packaging information and avoid these formulations), composted coir, coconut husks, bark, wood fibre, and green plant material, as well as rock minerals such as sand and clay, but you can easily make eco-friendly alternatives at home.

WHAT IS SOIL?

The organic matter we think of as compost is present in all good soils, but the soil itself is much more complex. Rocks, roots, decomposed plant material, soil-dwelling animals, and microorganisms are all found in a typical soil, but not all soils are the same. Discovering more about the type in your garden will help you to choose plants that will thrive there and to know how your compost can improve it.

The type of soil you have in your garden will determine which plants and crops will thrive there.

PLUMBING THE DEPTHS

Most people think of soil as the brown earthy material that plants grow in, and that is partly true. The crumbly or muddy material that comprises this upper layer, which is usually about 30–40cm (12–16in) deep, is known as "topsoil". Below that is "subsoil", which forms a deeper layer, reaching down 1.2m (4ft) or more into the ground. Beneath it is the bedrock on which soils form. Gardeners are mainly concerned with the fertile topsoil, where most plant growth occurs, but the subsoil also plays its part; it helps to store water and air for the long roots of larger plants, including trees and shrubs, to tap into. The bedrock influences the size of the soil particles. Known as its "texture", these determine whether the soil is free-draining or water-absorbent. The bedrock also affects a soil's acidity, alkalinity or neutrality.

Your garden soil is influenced by the bedrock and its organic matter content.

Plant leaves can increase soil moisture by limiting surface exposure to the sun ....

Compost and plant roots improve the soil structure ....

TOPSOIL

SUBSOIL

BEDROCK

The bedrock determines a soil's clay mineral content ....

HOW COMPOST AFFECTS THE SOIL

Compost is the magic ingredient that will improve the growing conditions in your garden, whatever the soil type (see *opposite*). The sticky black substance in compost known as "humus" coats sand and silt particles, helping them to retain more water and nutrients. In clay soils, it binds the tiny particles together to form larger aggregates with wider channels between them that allow air and water to pass through, thereby improving the soil's drainage capacity. Compost also attracts soil-borne creatures that feed on it, and they too open up passageways for water and air, as well as releasing plant nutrients via their faeces. Worms in particular are key to this process (see *p.23*). In addition, compost introduces microbes that increase fertility and support the growth of healthy plant roots, which also help to bind soils together, preventing erosion. All of these factors combine to create soils that hold water and nutrients, yet also drain well, providing the perfect conditions for plant growth.

SOIL TYPES

Soils are divided into three main groups: sand, silt, and clay. There are other soils that are not as widespread, such as chalk and peat, but these are rarely found in gardens. While all soils contain a combination of different ingredients, one sediment is often dominant. Soil that contains almost equal measures of sand and clay particles is known as "loam", which provides the perfect conditions for growing crops and many ornamental plants. However, there are plants that have adapted to all soil types, so you can still have a garden full of flowers and foliage if you do not have loam. You can also improve your soil by adding homemade compost, which will widen your planting choices.

SANDY SOILS These are made up of relatively large particles, which you can often see with the naked eye. The particles do not absorb moisture and there are comparatively wide gaps between them that allow water to drain through. This is why sandy soils dry out quickly, and because plant nutrients are dissolved in water, they also drain away, which makes these soils relatively infertile. Sandy soils also warm up quickly in spring but cool down just as fast in winter. They are easy to cultivate and are described as "light" for this reason, not because they are lighter in weight than other soils.

SILTY SOILS The particles in silt are smaller than sand but larger than clay. The gaps between them allow good drainage, but are small enough to hold some water and nutrients in the soil to boost fertility. Silty soils are not common in gardens and are generally found near rivers or in areas where rivers or seas previously existed.

CLAY SOILS These soils contain minute clay particles that can only be seen through a microscope. They are absorbent and the tiny gaps between them hold water in suspension rather than allowing it to drain through, which makes clay soils prone to waterlogging. They tend to be very fertile, but take longer than either sand or silt to warm up in spring. They also dry out and crack during the summer. They are described as "heavy" soils because they are difficult to dig.

Clay soil holds enough water to form a sticky ball when it is rolled in your hands.

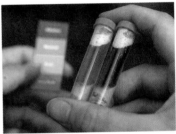

A soil-testing kit is an easy way to find out if your soil is acid, neutral, or alkaline.

TESTING YOUR SOIL

To find out which type of soil you have, take a sample about the size of a golf ball from just below the surface a few days after it has rained. Leave it to dry out until it is just damp, then rub it between your fingers. Sandy soil will feel gritty and when you try to roll it into a ball, it will fall apart. Silty soil feels slippery and will not form a solid ball either. Clay soil is sticky and smooth to the touch and will keep its shape, with a shiny surface, when rolled into a ball.

THE ACID TEST As well as knowing your soil's texture and structure, it is also important to establish its pH value, which is a measurement of its acidity, neutrality, or alkalinity. The pH value will influence your plant choices and it is easy to check using a soil-testing kit. Test a few samples taken from around the garden – you may find their values differ slightly in a large space. Dig up a sample from just below the surface and follow the instructions on the kit.

Drought-tolerant plants such as lavender, salvia, and thyme thrive in sandy soils.

Many fruit and vegetable crops will grow well in silty soils as long as they are free-draining.

NATURE'S COMPOST

Woodland ecosystems provide a great example of natural composting in action, so understanding the processes that occur in these environments offers a window into what takes place in your compost heap at home. You can also learn from the way in which decaying organic matter accumulates in layers and is incorporated into the soil by minibeasts, which help to maintain its delicate structure.

The woodland floor, and soil that lies beneath it, is teeming with minibeasts and microorganisms that decompose the tree leaves that fall each autumn.

NATURAL WOODLAND COMPOSTING

Composting at home is just a way of replicating what happens in a natural environment, but with more nitrogen-rich materials to speed up the process. The best way to see natural composting at work is to take a walk in a deciduous woodland. Explore the areas under the trees and you will see that the ground is covered with a layer of leaves that fell in autumn, known as "leaf litter". As well as this dead foliage, there will be twigs and green leaves, and perhaps branches that fell during a storm. In addition, you will find shrubs and other woodland plants benefiting from the dappled light shining through the tree canopies.

Scrape away the leaf litter and you will find a layer of partly decomposed leaves which fell in previous years. If you dig down into the soil, you may see small red worms, earthworms, and other minibeasts at work. Known as topsoil, this layer is dark in colour and includes decomposing plant material and minibeast faeces, along with fungi and bacteria that ingest the organic matter, converting some of it into plant nutrients. Worms and other creatures take this material down further into the subsoil to feed the roots there; this layer is paler in colour because it contains much lower levels of organic materials.

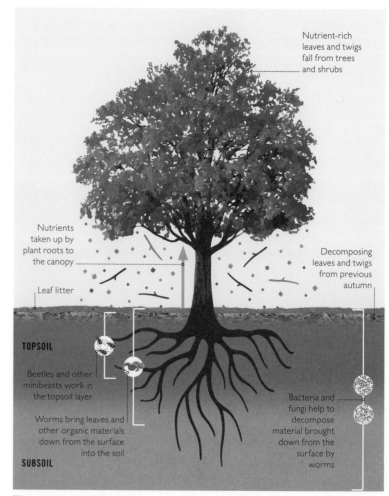

Nutrient-rich leaves and twigs fall from trees and shrubs

Nutrients taken up by plant roots to the canopy

Decomposing leaves and twigs from previous autumn

Leaf litter

TOPSOIL

Beetles and other minibeasts work in the topsoil layer

Worms bring leaves and other organic materials down from the surface into the soil

SUBSOIL

Bacteria and fungi help to decompose material brought down from the surface by worms

The autumn leaf drop perpetuates the formation of topsoil.

GRADUAL BREAKDOWN

Within the top 30cm (12in) or more of the soil, you will still see recognizable fragments of twigs and woody material; at this stage, the leaves will have degraded and become completely transformed. As you might expect, wood takes much longer to decompose than foliage, and the same holds true of the twigs and branches added to a compost heap. The remnants of trees may remain on a woodland floor or in the topsoil for many years before they completely decompose – a felled deciduous tree in a temperate woodland can take up to 70 years to rot down, while a conifer may take more than 120 years. Particular types of fungi and bacteria are needed in order to break down the tough material known as lignin that is present in wood and bark, and both operate more slowly than the bacteria which work on soft green leaves, stems, grasses, and most fruits and vegetables.

Fallen or felled branches take many years to fully decompose, during which time they play host to a wide range of minibeasts that feed on the rotting wood.

PLANT NUTRIENT RECYCLING

The growth of the trees and other plants in a woodland, and the conditions needed for seeds to germinate, are sustained by minibeasts and microorganisms in the soil. They recycle the nutrients in dead plant and animal material that enters the soil each year. Mycorrhizal fungi in particular play an important role by forming symbiotic relationships with plants. The fungi attach to the surface or grow inside roots and, in exchange for the carbon supplied by the plant, they deliver nutrients and water extracted from the soil. These fungi use carbon for energy. Bacteria also function as nutrient recyclers, as do many minibeasts, especially worms.

Trees and shrubs then enrich the upper layers of the soil by bringing mineral nutrients, such as nitrogen, from deep in the subsoil back up to the surface. The plants use these nutrients to form their leaf canopies, and return them to the soil when the foliage falls in autumn. The process of composting and recycling is slow – just 1cm (½in) of topsoil can take more than 1,000 years to form.

The nutrients released by microorganisms and minibeasts into the soil provide food for developing tree seedlings.

The soil in an ancient woodland will be much older than any of the trees, having been created over millennia. Some bulbs and fungi will also be older than the trees.

BENEFITING THE ENVIRONMENT

The compost you produce in your garden not only benefits the soil and feeds your plants, it also helps to create a healthier planet. Diverting green waste from landfill or incineration reduces air pollution and the greenhouse gases that contribute to global warming, while the compost itself helps to trap carbon in the soil. Organic matter improves the structure of soils, too, so that they retain water and nutrients more effectively. This lessens the need for artificial fertilizers, which cause pollution during their manufacture and when excess phosphates and nitrates leach into waterways.

Rotting food waste emits greenhouse gases that contribute to climate change.

REDUCING POLLUTANTS

Preventing kitchen and garden waste from going to landfill or incineration has huge benefits for the environment. In 2018, about 7.2 million tonnes of biodegradable green waste was sent to landfill in the UK, while the figure in the USA was 30 million tonnes. Burying this organic material is not another way of composting it, because when food and green waste are combined with other materials, oxygen is squeezed out and microorganisms that are not normally found in a compost heap start to decompose it (see also p.30). Known as anaerobic digestion, the process emits methane and carbon dioxide (CO_2) as byproducts – two greenhouse gases that contribute to global warming. The transport of green waste to landfill and incinerator sites also produces harmful pollutants.

LOCKING UP CARBON

While landfill generates greenhouse gases, compost has the opposite effect and actually helps to lock up carbon in the soil. The materials that are added to a compost heap are rich in carbon (see p.28), which plants extract from the air during photosynthesis, the process by which they produce food and energy. Some CO_2 is lost during decomposition, but the humus that forms once the composting is complete helps to trap carbon in the soil, ensuring it does not escape into the atmosphere. Another way compost helps to mitigate global warming is by aiding plant growth – more plants mean that greater volumes of CO_2 are absorbed from the air. Fungal mycorrhizas that live on and in plant roots also trap carbon (see p.15).

TOP TIP LAY COMPOST OVER THE SOIL AS A MULCH RATHER THAN DIGGING IT IN, WHICH BREAKS DOWN THE SOIL STRUCTURE AND RELEASES CO_2.

Compost helps to trap carbon in the soil and promotes lush plant growth, which captures CO_2 from the atmosphere.

An application of compost prevents topsoil from drying out in hot summers and being blown away on the wind.

Making your own potting mixes avoids buying products in plastic bags.

RENEWING SOILS

Soils take centuries to form, yet they can be eroded in a matter of months. In fact, the United Nations has estimated that the world loses 24 billion tonnes of fertile soil each year. While gardeners cannot change poor agricultural practices or prevent urbanization, we can play a small part in reducing soil erosion and our compost heaps will help us. Compost promotes good soil structures that trap water and support strong, healthy root growth that stabilizes them. These factors combine to prevent soils from being washed away during storms or eroded by wind during the summer when the upper layers become parched. Compost is also one of the building blocks of soil, helping to generate new topsoil. Some estimates suggest that homemade compost can create as much topsoil in a year as nature makes in a century.

REDUCING PLASTIC WASTE

Making your own compost means that you will not need to buy as many products contained in plastic bottles or packaging, especially if you use the contents of your bin or heap to make potting mixes (see pp.96–97). Applying homemade compost can also reduce the need for synthetic fertilizers, which produce many forms of pollution during their manufacture and transportation.

IMPROVING BIODIVERSITY

Compost is a rich source of food for a huge variety of soil-borne creatures, including springtails, nematodes, millipedes, and various types of worm. These in turn feed other invertebrates, such as centipedes, beetles, and spiders, which are preyed upon by larger creatures, including birds, frogs, toads, and foxes. Compost also creates ideal conditions for a wide range of plants that increase biodiversity. Pollen- and nectar-rich flowers draw in different species of bee, butterfly, and hoverfly, while berried shrubs and fruiting trees feed birds and small mammals. The plant life also offers sheltered conditions and protected habitats.

The worms that digest compost make a meal for other garden wildlife such as birds.

The minibeasts and microorganisms
responsible for composting are powered by
a diet rich in carbohydrates, which gives them
energy. They source food from materials such as
egg cartons, paper, and used potting compost.

COMPOSTING KNOW-HOW

Understanding how your organic matter breaks down is
the key to a successful compost heap or bin. The minibeasts
that feed on the raw waste you throw in need air and water
to survive, as do the bacteria and fungi that perform the
lion's share of the work and release plant nutrients into
the finished product. These decomposers also require
a balanced diet of foods rich in nitrogen and carbon, and
knowing which materials will supply these elements in
the right proportions helps you to make the rich, crumbly
compost that offers so many benefits in the garden.

THE COMPOSTING PROCESS

Composting helps to speed up the natural decomposition of organic material, a process that depends on the activity of billions of microorganisms and invertebrates that occur naturally in the soil. For rapid and efficient composting, your bin or heap should provide these organisms with the conditions they need to thrive – adequate warmth, moisture, and nutrient-rich food, as well as oxygen to breathe.

Fill your compost bin with a mixture of green and woody plant material.

HOW COMPOSTING WORKS

Composting is conducted by a range of minibeasts such as worms, millipedes, and beetles, together with a vast army of bacteria and fungi that are not visible to the naked eye. These organisms have differing requirements, and their activity also changes the conditions within a compost heap. The result is that different organisms are active at different times during decomposition. Understanding the processes at work in your bin will help you to produce compost as quickly and efficiently as possible. Scientists divide the composting process into three phases.

MESOPHILIC PHASE Larger creatures, such as worms and millipedes, break down organic matter by grinding, tearing, and chewing it into smaller pieces, making it more readily available for microorganisms to digest. Bacteria and fungi that thrive in warm temperatures of 20–45°C (68–113°F) are also present. They are known as mesophilic microbes because they operate in medium (meso) temperatures. As they work, these organisms produce heat, and within a few days, the temperature in the pile rises to over 40°C (104°F) and composting moves to the next phase.

THERMOPHILIC PHASE As temperatures in the compost heap increase, the conditions become too hot for worms

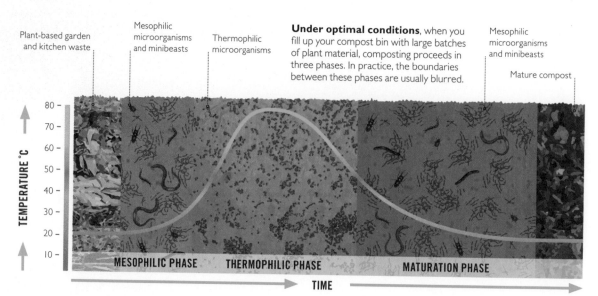

Plant-based garden and kitchen waste

Mesophilic microorganisms and minibeasts

Thermophilic microorganisms

Under optimal conditions, when you fill up your compost bin with large batches of plant material, composting proceeds in three phases. In practice, the boundaries between these phases are usually blurred.

Mesophilic microorganisms and minibeasts

Mature compost

TEMPERATURE °C

80 –
70 –
60 –
50 –
40 –
30 –
20 –
10 –

MESOPHILIC PHASE   **THERMOPHILIC PHASE**   **MATURATION PHASE**

TIME

and millipedes, which move out of the pile. The mesophilic microorganisms that kickstarted the process also die off or survive as thick-walled, heat-resistant spores. Thermophiles – organisms that thrive at high temperatures of 50–70°C (122–158°F) – then take over, breaking down energy-dense organic matter such as proteins, fats, and cellulose into chemical elements and compounds, including phosphorus, nitrogen, and potassium, that plants take up through their roots. The thermophilic phase can last from several days to several months, if food and air supplies are maintained.

MATURATION PHASE As the thermophilic microorganisms use up all the available high-energy organic matter, the compost starts to cool down, and decomposition is taken over by the mesophiles once again. Larger organisms, such as worms, mites, and slugs, return to the heap during this final phase, breaking down the compost further. Excreta from these creatures adds to the complex formation of the compost and its diverse nutrient content. The maturation stage can take months to convert or "cure" the remaining organic matter.

Large compost heaps can generate significant amounts of heat.

TURN UP THE HEAT

The hot thermophylic phase of the composting process is the key to producing compost quickly. It also kills off pests and diseases, which cannot survive the high temperatures. The traditional method, known as hot composting (see p.54–55), will achieve the heat required, but you need to supply the microbes and minibeasts with a large volume of food, delivered in one big batch, for it to work. The food fuels the decomposer activity needed to raise the temperature. To encourage thermophilic bacteria, the compost also needs to be well insulated so that the heat does not escape. Turning the compost regularly helps to sustain high temperatures too by supplying more oxygen to the microbes and exposing new organic material to their activity, which will increase the heat again when a bin starts to cool. Given these ideal conditions, compost can be produced in as little as 8–12 weeks.

If you have a small garden, you may find it difficult to collect large amounts of compostable material at one time, nor have space for a traditional hot bin, which needs to be big enough to hold it. This is not a cause for concern since heaps of organic matter that are built up over many months will eventually rot down and produce compost, although the thermophylic phase will not occur. Cooler processes take longer and the lower temperatures generated may not kill all the weed seeds and pests present in the compost.

WATER AND OXYGEN

Microorganisms need water to flourish, and if a heap becomes too dry, composting activity will stop altogether. Adding water to the heap in hot weather may help, but do so sparingly. Overwatering will displace oxygen and encourage organisms that function in airless (anaerobic) conditions over beneficial aerobic composters. It will also lower the temperature of the heap, suppressing the activities of the thermophiles. Remember, too, that dead plant material contains a high percentage of water and the process of decomposition releases it as a by-product. If a compost bin or heap is too wet, it will start to smell due to the ammonia and hydrogen sulphide that anaerobic microbes produce (see p.30).

Bins with lids prevent the compost from becoming too wet.

MINIBEAST COMPOSTERS

A whole host of tiny insects and invertebrates are present in the soil, and many find their way into compost bins, where they gorge on the plentiful food supply. They work alongside bacteria and fungi, shredding and eating the plant waste or preying upon other minibeasts in the heap. Some are microscopic and present in their millions, while others, such as centipedes, slugs, and beetles, are easy to spot.

Many types of worm live in a compost heap and their faeces (casts) help to increase the fertility of the final product.

HOW MINIBEASTS MAKE COMPOST

A compost heap teems with minibeasts which, together with microorganisms such as bacteria and fungi (see pp.24–25), eat the fresh and decaying plant debris and kitchen waste that you throw in, as well as dead animal matter and the faeces from other creatures living in the compost. The primary consumers are those that directly digest the organic matter, and they include mites, slugs, snails, woodlice, earthworms, and millipedes. They are preyed upon by other minibeasts, such as springtails, small beetles, nematodes, and soil flatworms, known as secondary consumers. At the top of the compost food web are the relative giants of the heap, the tertiary consumers, such as ants, carabid beetles, pseudoscorpions, and centipedes, which eat the primary and secondary consumers. These contribute to the heap by maintaining a balanced ecosystem and topping up the organic matter when they die. Together, these creatures help to make the crumbly compost that forms in your heap or bin.

COMPOST FOOD WEB

TERTIARY CONSUMERS (organisms that eat secondary consumers): rove beetles • centipedes • predatory mites • ants • carabid beetles • pseudoscorpions

SECONDARY CONSUMERS (organisms that eat primary consumers): springtails • mites • feather-winged beetles • nematodes • soil flatworms

PRIMARY CONSUMERS (organisms that eat organic materials): bacteria • fungi • actinomycetes • nematodes • mites • snails • slugs • earthworms • millipedes • woodlice

ORGANIC MATERIALS leaves • grass clippings • twigs • other plant debris • food scraps • animal faeces • dead bodies of compost-dwellers (such as worms and insects)

Woodlice work on tough, woody stems and provide food for other decomposers.

Most snails and slugs consume the fresh plant material that you throw into your bin.

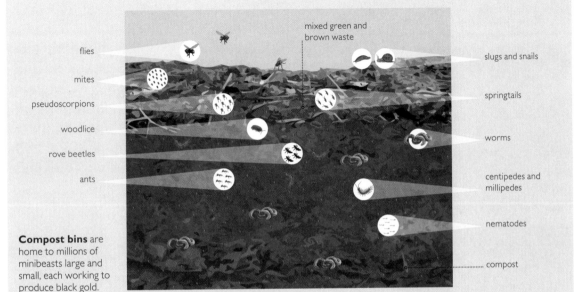

flies
mites
pseudoscorpions
woodlice
rove beetles
ants

mixed green and brown waste

slugs and snails
springtails
worms
centipedes and millipedes
nematodes
compost

Compost bins are home to millions of minibeasts large and small, each working to produce black gold.

BEASTS IN A HEAP

The following creatures are all at work in your compost heap. Some are too tiny to be seen without a microscope; others are a familiar sight in the garden.

WORMS These are among the most important composters. As well as the large pink earthworms found in gardens, there are brandling or red worms used in wormeries (see p.74–77), nematodes (see right), and potworms. All help to aerate the heap with their tunnelling, and they feed on dead plants and insects. Their excreta is very rich in plant nutrients and they help to neutralize the compost, making it more hospitable for other minibeasts and microbes.

ANTS As well as feeding on fungi, seeds, and insects in the compost, ants may also build nests there. Like worms, their tunnelling aerates the compost and they bring fungi and other microbes into their nests, which then release nutrients such as phosphorus and potassium.

BEETLES The most common species in compost are rove beetles, ground beetles, and feather-winged beetles. The tiny feather-winged species feed on fungi, while the larger rove and ground beetles prey on insects, slugs, snails, and other small creatures.

FLIES Adult fruit flies bring in useful bacteria when they fly into the heap and feed on the vegetation. House flies can be a nuisance and will lay their eggs in compost when the conditions are right. The maggots are killed by high temperatures, so they are less of a problem in hot heaps.

MILLIPEDES AND CENTIPEDES While millipedes eat decaying plants, dead insects, and excrement, centipedes are fast-moving predators at the top of the food web. They have claws behind their heads, through which they inject poison and paralyse their prey.

MITES The second most common invertebrate found in compost, some mite species consume leaves, wood, and other organic debris, while others

eat fungi. A few of them are tertiary consumers, feeding on nematodes, insect larvae, and springtails.

NEMATODES These microscopic worms make up the vast bulk of the minibeast decomposers – a handful of compost will contain several million. Various species are found in compost heaps, including primary consumers, and those that feed on bacteria and fungi.

PSEUDOSCORPIONS Resembling tiny scorpions, these creatures use the poison in their front claws to kill nematodes, mites, and small worms.

SLUGS AND SNAILS While most feed on living plants, a few of these molluscs feast on the dead materials in compost.

SPRINGTAILS Tiny wingless insects that jump when disturbed, springtails eat decomposing plants, fungi, nematodes, and the excreta of other arthropods.

WOODLICE Distant relatives of crabs, these crustaceans eat dead and decaying plant material in the compost.

BACTERIA AND FUNGI DECOMPOSERS

Most of the composting that takes place in your bin is conducted by microbes that are invisible to the naked eye. These microorganisms are naturally occurring in the soil and will arrive in your compost heap via the garden waste you add to it. They require air and water, as well as a good supply of food, to create compost, and will work faster when you can provide these optimum conditions in your pile.

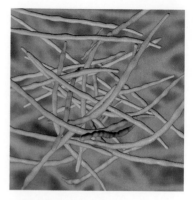

Actinomycete bacteria form fungus-like strands in compost that look like spiders' webs. They feed on tough woody material such as shrub stems.

There are billions of microorganisms in just a pinch of garden soil.

MICROBE COMPOSTING

Billions of microorganisms are needed to transform your kitchen and garden waste into crumbly compost. Together with an army of minibeasts (see pp.22–23), bacteria, fungi, and other microbes break down the organic matter in a heap and release the nutrients that plants need for growth. They also help to establish a healthy ecosystem in the compost and are eaten by some of the insects and invertebrates in the heap.

BACTERIA AT WORK

It is essential to give the beneficial bacteria in your compost heap the conditions they need, since they make up 90 per cent of the microorganism decomposers, working mainly on the green materials (see p.33). Bacteria can be divided into two types: "aerobic" bacteria breathe in oxygen, while "anaerobic" bacteria operate without it. Aerobic bacteria produce sweet-smelling compost, but if the mix becomes wet and airless, anaerobic bacteria take over. While they also break down organic matter, anaerobes produce harmful gases that cause the compost to smell and pollute the atmosphere (see p.30). The compost they make is also too acidic to benefit most plants, so make sure air is flowing through your heap to keep the good bacteria thriving.

Actinomycetes are a different type of bacteria that digest woody waste, rather than green materials. They break down tough stems and bark, mainly during the maturation stage of the composting process, although some are present when the contents are hot. They produce fungal-like growths that look like whitish-grey spiders' webs, which you may see threaded through the compost material as it matures.

THE FUNCTION OF FUNGI

Fungi are not as numerous as bacteria, but perform an equally important role by breaking down the woody material that many other microbes find hard to digest. They produce fungal strands in the compost, some of which are too small to see, while others appear as grey or white growths on the surface. These bind compost particles together, creating passageways for air to travel through. Most fungi operate when the compost is warm, but a few are active in the thermophilic phase (see pp.20–21).

Fungal strands help to bind compost particles together, which improves air flow.

NEED TO KNOW
- The bacteria in compost and the soil can be very beneficial, helping to increase our immunity against some diseases. To ensure your heap is filled with good bacteria, do not allow it to become waterlogged, nor include cat and dog faeces.
- There are many different forms of fungi. Some help to decompose the contents of your compost bin, others form symbiotic relationships with plants' roots and supply them with the nutrients needed to sustain healthy growth.

Kitchen and garden waste can both go on the compost heap, where they will eventually break down into valuable compost.

FEEDING THE DECOMPOSERS

The minibeasts and microorganisms in the compost pile require nutritious foods to perform their functions. Providing them with plenty of energy-giving carbohydrates and health-promoting proteins, as well as vitamins and minerals, will keep them working efficiently. By keeping the decomposers well fed you will also be providing food for larger creatures such as toads, which eat them in turn.

Layer the carbs and protein-rich foods in your bin to produce the perfect "sandwich" for microbes and minibeasts.

Balancing the contents in compost is compared to making a cheese sandwich.

A BALANCED DIET

Just like humans, the inhabitants of your compost heap thrive on a balanced diet. The minibeasts and microbes require carbohydrates (compounds of carbon, hydrogen, and oxygen) for energy, proteins to build and repair cells, and vitamins and minerals to keep them healthy. Compost experts describe the perfect recipe for decomposers as being like a cheese sandwich: you need carb-heavy bread and protein-rich cheese, perhaps with slightly more bread for a good balance. The air-filled bread also complements the denser composition of the cheese to form an agreeable structure. The same is true of a compost heap, where layers of carbon- and nitrogen-rich materials create the optimum conditions.

ENERGY SOURCES

The carbohydrates in a compost heap come from woody materials such as twigs, straw, autumn leaves, and bark, as well as household items, including paper and card. The surface area of these carbon-rich foods determines how quickly they will be ingested by the decomposers – for example, fungi and actinomycetes (see p.24) consume paper and card, which have large surface areas, faster than woody stems. The plant materials also contain tough cellulose and lignin that take the microbes longer to process. The decomposers release carbon dioxide (CO_2) through respiration, just like we do; about two-thirds of the carbon is lost in this way, while a third remains stored in the compost.

TOP TIP SPEED UP THE COMPOSTING PROCESS BY CHOPPING OR SHREDDING WOODY WASTE SUCH AS TREE AND SHRUB PRUNINGS. DO NOT COMPOST LOGS — INSTEAD, STACK THEM UP IN A QUIET CORNER TO CREATE A WILDLIFE HABITAT.

Woody prunings will be packed with carbohydrates that decomposers such as fungi use for energy.

Kitchen scraps provide the decomposers with the proteins they need to grow and reproduce.

PROTEIN POWER

Cell repair and growth is powered by proteins, which the decomposers find in soft green plant material such as grass clippings, young leaves, flowers, and weed seedlings, together with kitchen peelings, cooked vegetables, animal manure, and dead insects and other minibeasts that inhabit the compost heap. These materials also contain a rich supply of vitamins and minerals, some of which are processed by the decomposers and released into the compost as plant nutrients. Not surprisingly, the more varied the ingredients you throw into your bin, the wider the range of nutrients will come out of it.

WASHING IT DOWN WITH WATER

Bacteria and fungi, which perform the lion's share of the decomposing in your bin, live in a thin film of water that covers the compost particles. The minibeasts also require water and will die if your heap dries out, so make sure that the ingredients are damp, but not waterlogged – a soggy heap will drown these creatures and push out the air they need to breathe (see p.21) Leafy plants and kitchen scraps usually contain enough moisture to keep the decomposers in a compost heap happy.

Even when uprooted, grass and leafy plants contain sufficient water to keep the decomposers in your bin healthy.

SUPPLY AND DEMAND

Just as all animals, including humans, need a constant supply of food to live, so the decomposers in your heap also require a stream of ingredients to keep them active. That does not mean you have to add materials daily or even weekly, since the average compost heap can provide food for decomposers for many months (or even a year if it is a cool heap). Most people with just one heap include ingredients in batches, which means that the top layers may not be fully digested by the minibeast-microbe populations when the bottom layers that have been worked on are ready to use. You can put this undigested material to one side when you remove the mature compost, and then simply add it to the empty bin to be processed with your next batch of ingredients. The finished compost will still include organic matter in which soil microbes and some minibeasts are still active, which is why it is really a matter of opinion as to when the process is complete.

The microbes in your compost heap need a plentiful supply of food from the garden and kitchen.

KEY ELEMENTS FOR COMPOSTING

Gardeners do not require a chemistry degree to make good compost, but a little understanding of the role of key elements such as nitrogen and carbon can help to deliver better results. These are found in the materials you add to a bin and are not only digested by microbes and minibeasts, but also help to maintain a well-aerated structure when added in the correct proportions.

Plants contain varying quantities of key elements such as nitrogen and carbon, which are needed for efficient composting.

WHAT IS CARBON?

Plants contain large quantities of carbon, as do animals, including humans. To obtain it, plants take carbon dioxide (CO_2) from the atmosphere during the day and use it, together with water and energy from sunlight, to produce food and sustain their growth in a process known as photosynthesis. The by-product of this chemical reaction is oxygen, which plants release into the atmosphere. We humans and other animals then breathe in the oxygen and exhale carbon dioxide.

While carbon can be found in all parts of a plant, it is more concentrated in the woody areas, such as the stems, branches, and bark. Mature tree leaves are also rich sources. When a plant dies, most of the carbon it contains is lost as carbon dioxide (CO_2) during decomposition, but the remainder is fixed in the soil by the minibeasts and microbes, which is why compost is considered a carbon sink and helps to mitigate the effects of climate change (see pp.16–17). Living plants also release carbon from their roots, which is taken up by microorganisms such as fungi and used for energy.

Carbon is found in large quantities in the wood, bark, and leaves of trees.

Runner bean plants take nitrogen from the air and store it in nodules on their roots.

WHY IS NITROGEN NEEDED?

Nitrogen is one of the main nutrients plants need for healthy growth. It is a major component of chlorophyll, which gives leaves and stems their green colour and allows them to make food through photosynthesis. In the air as nitrogen gas (N_2), it is more prevalent than oxygen and makes up 78 per cent of the Earth's atmosphere (oxygen accounts for 21 per cent). Some plants, including peas and beans, are able to extract nitrogen from the air and store it in nodules on their roots, which then feed the plant. However, most draw it up through their roots in a solution from the soil.

In a compost heap, nitrogen fuels the activity of the microbes and helps them to build the proteins they need to support growth and reproduction. The soft, leafy green plants and kitchen waste you add to your compost pile are good sources of nitrogen.

THE CARBON-TO-NITROGEN RATIO

Compost experts often talk about the carbon-to-nitrogen ratio of the materials that are included in a heap. Usually abbreviated to the C:N ratio, this simply means the proportion of carbon to nitrogen contained in the items. For example, grass clippings have a C:N ratio of about 20:1, which means they have 20 times as much carbon as nitrogen. Tree leaves have a ratio of 50:1, so they contain more carbon than grass, while wood and paper may have a ratio of 100:1 up to 500:1. The ideal C:N ratio for a healthy compost heap is about 30:1 (*see also p.32–33*).

If ratio numbers don't appeal, you can just go by appearance. The parts of a plant that are soft, lush, and green – and therefore have more nitrogen – will have a low C:N ratio, while woody waste will have a high C:N ratio. Layering nitrogen- and carbon-rich materials will achieve a good mix.

The lush, leafy stems of nasturtiums have a relatively low C:N ratio compared to woody twigs.

TOP TIP YOU CAN TEST THE PH (ACIDITY) OF YOUR COMPOST USING A SOIL-TESTING KIT. IF IT IS ACIDIC, INTRODUCING MORE AIR TO REACTIVATE THE MICROBES, ALONG WITH SOME CALCIUM-RICH PLANTS, WILL HELP TO NEUTRALIZE IT.

CALCIUM MATTERS

The bacteria in a compost heap produce organic acids, which are broken down further by other microorganisms and worms that help to neutralize the mix. If there is not much oxygen in the heap, microbes that function in anaerobic conditions take over and create acidic compost. While some plants, such as heathers and rhododendrons, thrive in acid soil, (*see p.13*), most prefer neutral or slightly alkaline soils, and the decomposer bacteria also dislike acidity. Calcium is alkaline, so adding plants that are good sources of it will help to neutralize an acidic heap. Brassica leaves and stalks, seaweed, and the leaves of ash, cherry, lime, hawthorn, and roses are all good sources of calcium, as are eggshells.

The leaves of cherry trees are rich in calcium and help to neutralize acid compost.

BALANCING AIR AND WATER

The decomposers in your heap breathe in oxygen and exhale carbon dioxide, so it is vital to keep air flowing through it. They also need moisture, and some microbes live in a thin film of water. To make compost successfully, create a balance of air and water by limiting the volume of moisture-rich materials, such as vegetables and grass, which can quickly lose structure and create inhospitable, airless conditions if added in excess.

Turning the contents of your compost will introduce air but can be hard work.

Well-aerated heaps will draw large populations of earthworms.

WHY IS AIR IMPORTANT?

The composting creatures and microbes in your heap all need oxygen to work as you want them to. When all the air in a heap is used up, the minibeasts die or move out and the microorganisms are replaced by bacteria that respire anaerobically (without oxygen). These will continue to break down the waste material, albeit more slowly, but produce unwanted by-products, including methane, carbon dioxide, ammonia, and hydrogen sulphide. Methane and carbon dioxide are two of the greenhouse gases responsible for global warming, while ammonia and hydrogen sulphide are toxic and will produce bad odours that no one wants in their garden.

HOW TO KEEP OXYGEN FLOWING

A good way to keep your compost sweet and filled with air is to turn over the contents of your bin to introduce more oxygen. If you have the space and strength to do this, it will invigorate the various decomposers and help to produce compost quickly and efficiently. However, turning the materials can be hard work and it may also be difficult to achieve in a small garden; you will need to empty the bin out every week or two, mix up all of the contents and then put them back. Alternatively, you could try just stirring the contents with a fork, but this too requires quite a lot of muscle-power.

If you have a smaller garden and not much spare time or energy, a more practical option is to create air pockets in the heap by adding a range of woody or paper-based materials as you go along. Compost piles often become anaerobic when an excess of green waste, such as grass clippings or kitchen scraps, rots down quickly, forming an airless, soupy sludge. To prevent this, start off your heap with a layer of twigs or small branches on the base to allow air to filter in from the bottom. When you are filling up the bin, include more twigs, plus scrunched-up newspaper, cardboard boxes, the inner tubes of toilet tissue, and eggboxes, along with your green waste. These wood and paper materials inject oxygen into the mix, keeping the composters working well and preventing odours.

Lining the base of a compost heap with twigs and small branches allows ventilation.

Apples and other fruits consist of more than 80 per cent water, which is released when they are added to a compost heap.

WATER NEEDS IN THE COMPOST HEAP

Compost minibeasts and microbes require water to live (see *pp.26-27*), but how do you know whether your bin has the right amount of moisture for their needs? In a perfect compost heap, water will account for 50–60 per cent of the total weight, which means that for every piece of dry cardboard you add, you need to include roughly the same quantity of water. This is obviously quite difficult to measure out in reality, but there is a simple method of maintaining a good moisture content.

The first step is to ensure that your heap is well insulated so that water does not evaporate and dry out the contents too quickly. Then limit the volume of kitchen scraps, soft green garden waste, and grass clippings that you add at any one time, as they will introduce too much moisture and drive out the air. These materials are made up of about 80 per cent water or more, which will be released into the heap as the decomposers get to work on them. Supplement your green stuff with porous brown materials such as paper and card products – the same ingredients, in fact, that also help to aerate the bin (see *opposite*).

You can test the moisture content of the heap by taking a handful of compost from the middle and squeezing it in your hand – a few drops of water should come out if it has the right amount. If the compost feels too wet, add more browns to it; if it is too dry, include more green materials (see also *pp.32–33*).

EXCESS GREEN WASTE

If you have too much green waste, consider creating two bins where you have space and enough woody material to mix with it in the second one. Alternatively, leave it out for kerbside collection, if your council provides a green waste bin, or take it to a municipal recycling centre. It will then be used to make compost or added to an industrial anaerobic digester, the gases from which are siphoned off for methane-rich biogas. This is used in combined heat and power (CHP) plants to produce electricity and heat, and no methane is released into the atmosphere.

RECIPES FOR SUCCESS

You can put most garden and kitchen waste on your compost heap, as you would expect, but also household items such as newspapers and magazines, which help to balance out any excesses of soft green waste that can make a heap smell and lose its structure. Getting to know the effects that different ingredients can have on your heap will help you to produce the best compost in the shortest time.

Most garden waste can be added to your heap, from bedding plants to prunings from shrubs and trees.

Kitchen waste such as fruit, vegetables, seeds, and eggshells is ideal content for the compost heap.

The bedding of guinea-pigs and similar small rodent pets will enrich your compost with carbon and nitrogen.

WASTE NOT, WANT NOT

Any plant-based food scraps that you would normally put into a bin for kerbside collection can be added to your compost heap instead. These include fruit and vegetable peelings and cores, stale or mouldy bread and biscuits, rice, barley, pasta, noodles, eggshells, and corn cobs, which will all make a good meal for the decomposers in your pile. Deter vermin from raiding your heap by ensuring that your bin is securely covered after you have added

cooked items such as bread and pasta, and push them down into the centre of the heap to disguise their smell.

While cardboard and paper, including newspaper and magazines, can go in, do not add them in large amounts as they have a very high carbon ratio (see *opposite*). You can even add the detritus from a vacuum cleaner, if it does not

contain plastics, as well as nail clippings and hair from pets and your brush. Pure cotton and wool products are acceptable in minor quantities, but cut them up into small pieces first. Rabbit, guinea pig, and hamster bedding can all go in too. However, do not add meat, fish, dairy products, or fats (for more on what not to add to your heap, see *pp.33–35*).

> **TOP TIP** FRUIT PEELS AND TOUGH STEMS SUCH AS THOSE OF BRASSICAS AND CORN COBS WILL DECOMPOSE MORE QUICKLY IF YOU CHOP THEM UP WITH A KNIFE OR SMASH THEM WITH A HAMMER TO BREAK THEM DOWN. THIS WILL CREATE A GREATER SURFACE AREA FOR THE DECOMPOSERS TO GET TO WORK ON.

GARDEN SUPPLIES

Almost anything from the garden can go in the compost heap, but large, woody stems will take a long time to decompose and are best used elsewhere (see pp.68–69). Dead flowers, pruned perennial plant and green shrub stems, annual weeds that have not flowered or set seed (see p.39), roots, old bedding plants, used compost from pots and containers, and fallen fruits will all help to make a rich, crumbly compost. Most of the waste from the vegetable garden, such as old cabbage leaves and stems, is ideal for a compost bin too.

Tree leaves that fall in autumn are rich in carbon but take a long time to decompose in a mixed compost heap.

You can add thin layers to your pile, but it is often best to compost large volumes of foliage separately to make leafmould (see pp.66–67). Also take care not to add many poisonous leaves from plants such as oleander (*Nerium oleander*), hemlock (*Conium maculatum*), black walnut (*Juglans nigra*), and the caster oil plant (*Ricinus communis*), which can harm creatures in the compost and in the soil when included in large quantities. Waxy leaves, such as those of magnolia, laurel, and rhododendrons, decay extremely slowly, so chop them up before adding them to your compost bin.

Dead flowerheads are perfect for increasing nitrogen levels and speeding up the composting process.

COLOUR CODING YOUR WASTE

The ideal carbon to nitrogen (C:N) ratio (see p.29) of a compost heap is about 30:1 – often referred to as simply 30 – so it may seem obvious that you will need to add more carbon-rich items than those with a high nitrogen content. However, this is not as simple as it sounds, because organic materials contain both elements, and almost all have more carbon than nitrogen – some even have a perfect ratio of 30:1. Get to know your waste a little better so that you can tell at a glance the "green" items that are rich in nitrogen, which include plants with soft leaves, stems, flowers, and fruits, and the tough, woody "browns" that contain larger volumes

of carbon. This allows you to divide up your materials by simply looking at their overall colour or feeling their texture.

The tables (see right) give you an idea of the C:N ratio of some of the most common compostable household and garden items. They are presented in order of carbon content, so products with the most carbon are listed at the top and those with the least are at the bottom. Although no gardener is expected to memorize the exact ratios of all the materials they add to a heap, you can see generally where most items stand. For more details of different composting methods and how to mix these items successfully, see pp.54–65.

BROWNS = HIGH CARBON CONTENT

BROWN WASTE	C:N RATIO
Wood chips	700
Sawdust	500
Cardboard	350
Newspaper	175
Straw/hay	90
Pine needles	60–80
Nutshells	35

GREENS = HIGH NITROGEN CONTENT

GREEN WASTE	C:N RATIO
Green garden	30
Fruit	25–40
Clover	23
Coffee grounds	20
General food	20
Grass clippings	20
Rotted animal manures	20
Annual weeds	20
Vegetable	12–25

Dividing up your waste into greens and browns makes it easy to achieve a good balance of ingredients.

WHAT NOT TO COMPOST

The list of products that are best left out of a heap is quite short and easy to remember. Plants that have been treated with pesticides and herbicides are not recommended, since these chemicals may kill both your decomposers and your plants. Pernicious weeds and plants showing signs of disease, or those that might be harbouring pests, should also be excluded from the average garden heap, which will not heat up sufficiently to kill them. An easy rule of thumb for other waste is to leave out meat, fish, eggs, and dairy items, and products that contain man-made materials such as plastics.

Ash and coals from a barbecue may contain toxic chemicals, so leave them out.

ANIMAL PRODUCTS

While meat, fish, and eggs will biodegrade in a compost heap, they will also attract flies and vermin such as rats. To avoid problems, put these items out for kerbside collection or add them to a bokashi bin (see p.78–81). Dairy products and fats, such as butter and vegetable oils, should be banished for similar reasons and also because they disrupt the natural composting process – they coat other particles with a greasy layer that displaces water and reduces the air flow needed for decomposers to work efficiently. Add fats and oils to other non-compostable food waste for kerbside or municipal recycling where they can be treated safely.

Meat and fatty sauces may attract vermin or inhibit the composting process.

Glossy wrapping paper may contain toxic chemicals that harm decomposers.

NON-BIODEGRADABLE MATERIALS

It may seem obvious to keep plastics and other non-biodegradable materials out of your heap, but some are not easy to spot. Cardboard used for juice, milk, and sandwich cartons is laminated with a plastic coating, and while magazines can be included in your heap, glossy finishes on covers, cards, and wrapping paper make some of these items unsuitable. Tea leaves are perfect for inclusion,

Check packaging to make sure your teabags do not contain plastic.

but tea bags may contain hidden plastics that will not decompose. Many tea companies have removed plastics from their products, but check the packs before composting. Keeping plastics out of your bin is imperative because research shows that microplastics affect the wellbeing of composting creatures such as springtails and mites. Some wet wipes are technically biodegradable but can take a very long time to rot down and are best left out, as are any products containing glass or metal, which will not biodegrade and may also contain toxic chemicals.

Create a logpile for wildlife rather than composting large prunings, which would take too long to break down.

NATURAL NO-NOS

Large branches or logs will take too long to decompose if you add them to your heap without shredding them first. Even then, the wood chips will have a high carbon content that may create a very dry and unproductive heap if they are included in large quantities. Alternative uses for logs include making them into a wood pile in the garden, which will help to support wildlife such as hibernating mammals and amphibians as well as beetles that feed on dead wood, or cutting and stacking them up to create low walls for a raised bed. Any other excess wood can be taken to your local municipal recycling centre, where it can be composted more effectively.

Charcoal and ash from your barbecue are other natural products to leave out of a heap because they contain chemicals including sulphur dioxide (SO_2) that will harm worms and other decomposers. Experts also warn against adding lime, which is sometimes recommended to neutralize an acidic heap, but may make your compost too alkaline instead. It is better to simply add plants and scraps that contain good sources of calcium to create a well-balanced compost mix (see p.29).

NEED TO KNOW
- Do not include cat, dog, or human faeces in your bin. They not only smell bad but may also carry disease pathogens that only the hottest of bins will kill.
- Leave out disposable nappies, which contain plastic as well as human waste.
- You can add human urine provided it is not derived from anyone who is taking medication. In healthy people, urine is sterile and has a high nitrogen content that can help to kick-start a sluggish heap.

USING ANIMAL MANURES

For thousands of years, animal manures have been used to improve soil fertility and boost crop production. The dung from livestock, horses, and even domesticated pigeons is all useful and provides a rich source of nitrogen that helps to activate the microbe decomposers when it is added to a compost heap. Many gardeners also use manures to bulk up their own plant-based materials to create enough ingredients for a hot bin (see pp.54–55). Alternatively, you can combine animal dung with straw and compost it separately to make a slow-release fertilizer and soil conditioner.

THE BENEFITS OF MANURES

Animal manures have many benefits for the home gardener and were the main source of extra food for plants until chemical fertilizers were introduced in the early 20th century. While animal manures contain some nutrients, such as phosphorous and potassium, in smaller quantities than most garden compost mixes, they behave in a similar way when applied to the soil, delivering their goodness slowly over time and allowing plants to take up the food when it is needed.

Fresh manure can burn plant roots and it is generally only used as a mulch on soil in autumn, where it will break down over winter and early spring before the planting season starts. Well-rotted manure (see opposite) helps to build stable soils that hold water well, while allowing excess moisture to drain away easily. When manures are used in a compost heap, their high nitrogen content feeds microbes and can help to speed up the decomposition process; the addition of poultry or pigeon manure is often recommended to kick-start a sluggish heap.

Well-rotted animal manures will boost the nitrogen content of your compost heap.

Horse manure contains the perfect balance of plant nutrients.

Pig manure may contain parasites if the animals are not well cared for.

WORDS OF WARNING

Not all manures will deliver benefits to your soil and plants. Never use faeces from cats and dogs, which have few plant nutrients and may contain pathogens. The safety of other manures can be compromised if used fresh and if they are not sourced from certified organic farms and stables. To prevent products contaminated with herbicides from killing your plants and crops, ask your supplier if they can guarantee that their animals have been fed on crops grown organically and that these harmful chemicals have not been used on any straw mixed with the manure.

Pig and other animal manures may contain parasites such as roundworms, although the risk is relatively low where they have been acquired from a reliable source with a good animal husbandry record. There is also a slight risk that manures will be contaminated with diseases such as E. coli and salmonella, and fresh manures should never be used on edible crops that will be eaten raw. To prevent these problems and make manure safe, compost it before use. Composting also reduces the high levels of nitrogen in fresh manure which can burn plant roots when it is applied directly to the soil.

Using too much manure on your garden can lead to an excess of nutrients that have not been taken up by your plants leaching into the ground water and polluting waterways. To avoid this, do not apply large quantities to the soil in autumn.

CHOOSING MANURES

Cow, sheep, goat, horse, and poultry manures are the safest choices for the home gardener – those from horses, sheep, and goats contain the best balance of the main plant nutrients. Poultry and pigeon manures are very high in nitrogen and should only be added to a compost heap in very small quantities. Use manure sourced from domesticated pigeons; if you do not own any, ask friends who keep them if they can spare some used bedding, but never collect wild pigeon manure, which may contain dangerous pathogens.

Keeping your own chickens will provide a source of valuable manure.

USING MANURES

Unless your supplier can guarantee that their products are well-rotted, stack manure and straw mixes under tarpaulin or similar waterproof material in a corner of the garden to decompose for at least six months (or longer if stacked over winter). The manure will undergo the same composting process as your heap, heating up quickly and then cooling down (see pp.20–21). If it fails to heat up, add some more straw or cardboard, which will increase the carbon content and introduce more air into the mix. Rotted manure is safe to use as a mulch or in potting mixes instead of compost when it smells sweet.

Alternatively, add thin layers of fresh or rotted manure to your compost heap to provide a nitrogen fix for the decomposers. Remember to wear gloves when handling fresh manure and wash your hands thoroughly after applying well-rotted dung.

Stack fresh manure mixed with straw for at least six months to rot down.

TOP TIP MAKE A HOTBED FOR TENDER CROPS, SUCH AS TOMATOES, USING A PILE OF COMPOSTING MANURE COVERED WITH A 10–15CM (4–6IN) LAYER OF ROTTED GARDEN COMPOST. THE FRESH DUNG MIX WILL HEAT UP AND THEN COOL DOWN TO BELOW 25°C (77°F), AT WHICH POINT YOU CAN PLANT INTO THE COMPOST ON TOP.

DEALING WITH WEEDS, PESTS, AND DISEASES

Hot composting will destroy many pests and diseases, but the average garden heap rarely reaches the high temperatures needed. The answer is to be vigilant and check the materials you plan to add for signs of disease or pest pupae. Also identify the weeds in your garden so that you know which can be safely included in your bin, rather than inadvertently spreading weeds that survive composting all over your plot.

Pernicious weeds such as bindweed can survive in a cool compost heap.

Seedlings hoed off before flowering are safe to add to a compost heap.

WEED WISDOM

You can hoe off annual weeds such as groundsel, chickweed, and bittercress before they flower or set seed and add them to the compost heap, whichever method you are using. Untreated perennial weeds such as bramble and bindweed should not be included unless you can guarantee the high temperatures reached using the hottest composting method (see pp.54–55). This is because these pernicious plants will survive cooler conditions and can regrow from even the tiniest piece of viable root or stem.

The only way to safely include pernicious weeds in a cool compost heap is to treat them first, so that they do not regrow. Dig out the weeds with as much of their rootball as possible, then lay them out in the sun during a dry spell, away from other plants – on a patio for example – and leave them for a week or so to shrivel up. Drowning them in water for a week should also kill off any signs of life. Another option is to bag them up tightly to exclude all light and put them aside for a year to decompose – though this may not be practical if you have a lot of weeds to dispose of.

SEEDING PROBLEMS

Many weed seeds will find their way into an open-topped heap, even if you do not add them attached to the parent plants. A cover will reduce this risk, as will allowing the compost to mature for longer; the more time seeds spend in a compost heap, even those that do not reach high temperatures, the more will die, because most will have been eaten by worms whose digestive systems will kill them. Some seeds can survive but many gardeners accept this, since weeds will arrive in a garden anyway and the loose structure of compost usually makes them easier to remove.

Seeds from weeds such as groundsel are killed as they pass through the digestive systems of worms.

KEEPING DISEASE AT BAY

While many of the diseases that afflict plants will be killed by the high temperatures in a hot compost heap, they may survive in cooler piles. Plants affected by viruses, which cause streaked and mosaic patterns on the foliage and flowers, should be omitted. Diseases such as root rots and honey fungus that thrive under the soil will probably survive life in the average garden compost heap, so plants carrying them should also not be added to a cool heap.

However, a few diseases can be safely included in a bin, such as plants affected by black spot, mildews, grey mould, and potato and tomato blights. It may seem counter-intuitive to add blight, but this fungus-like disease cannot survive on dead plant material, so the compost heap is a good place to dispose of infected crops. Take care not to spread the infection before composting by washing hands and equipment thoroughly after handling blighted material.

As with weed seeds, the longer you leave a pile, the less likely infections will survive the process – but if you cannot identify a disease afflicting a plant, it is probably best to leave it out. The easily recognizable diseases that you can or cannot safely add to your heap are shown below.

DISEASES TO ADD

Black spot   **Mildew**   **Grey mould**   **Tomato blight**   **Brown rot**

DISEASES TO LEAVE OUT

Rusts   **Root rot**   **Honey fungus**   **Clubroot**   **Viral diseases**

PEST ATTACKS

Plants that have been eaten by pests such as slugs and aphids can be thrown on to a compost pile – molluscs will already be living in most heaps, so it will make little difference if you add a few more. Also include plants affected by leaf miners, which do little damage anyway. The pupae of many pests, including carrot and cabbage root fly, have tough shells and may well survive in a cool compost bin, so check your plants for them beforehand.

To prevent vermin such as rats and mice from invading your bin, do not add meat, fish, or dairy produce, and push any cooked leftovers into the centre of the pile so they are surrounded by less appetising waste (see also p.34–35).

TOP TIP BINS CAN BECOME INFESTED WITH FLIES, WHICH ARE ATTRACTED TO THE FOOD WASTE. TO HELP PREVENT THIS, COVER YOUR KITCHEN SCRAPS WITH A BARRIER OF CARDBOARD, SOIL, OR WOODY GARDEN WASTE TO DISGUISE THEIR SMELL.

Cabbage root fly pupae will survive the conditions in a cool compost heap.

A small compost bin needs careful management, with plenty of brown waste to mop up the moisture from kitchen scraps, and the patience to wait for up to a year for your finished product.

MAKING COMPOST

There are many ways to make compost and the method you choose will depend on the size of your garden, the amount and type of material you have to fill a bin, and how long you are prepared to wait for your black gold. The techniques described in this chapter will help you to find a method that suits your circumstances, and if your outdoor space is limited, you can even choose to make compost indoors. Simply follow the instructions carefully and you will soon be harvesting homemade compost to boost your garden's performance.

BIN BASICS

Any structure that insulates your food and garden waste and prevents rain from washing away its valuable nutrients will make good compost, though some designs will help to produce it more quickly than others. Homemade bins, especially those made from wood, can be just as effective as manufactured models, and will help to reduce your carbon footprint. Remember, too, that the composting method you use can influence the speed at which your waste decomposes, and the texture of the final compost, just as much as the type of bin you choose.

Homemade bins that provide good insulation and air flow will be as effective as manufactured models.

BINS VS HEAPS

There are many different ways to make compost and the process will work with or without a bin. You can simply pile up your waste in a heap in a quiet area of the garden, partially cover it with a waterproof material, and leave it for a year or more to decompose. However, bins or structures of some sort do have a few key advantages. They look neater and are easier to manage in most garden settings, and they insulate the composting material, which speeds up decomposition, since heat accelerates the work of the microorganisms (see p.21). A protected environment also allows more composting to take place when temperatures outside the bin are too low for decomposers to be active.

Closed bins, such as the plastic models widely available through local authority schemes, will provide some insulation but not much air flow, which is needed for the decomposers to perform their function. To introduce more air into this type of bin, add ingredients such as scrunched-up newspaper or cardboard, egg cartons, and twiggy material, or turn or stir the contents regularly.

Wooden bins tend to offer better insulation than plastic models, although you will still need to introduce air in the same ways for quicker results. Bins with large gaps around the sides will have too much air flowing through them, causing the contents to cool down in winter and dry out quickly in warm weather, which will inhibit the actions of the decomposers and thus decelerate progress. However, even when the conditions are not perfect in a bin or heap, given enough time, the waste material in it will eventually decompose and form the rich compost you want for use in your garden.

Add scrunched-up newspapers and egg cartons to closed bins to introduce more air into the compost.

SELECTING A SIZE

For the most efficient composting, your bin should measure 1 cubic metre (1 cubic yard), which equates to a capacity of about 1000 litres (250 US gallons). This size is recommended because it effectively insulates the compost in the centre of the bin, allowing the microbes to flourish. The drawbacks are that you will need the space to accommodate a large bin and enough materials to fill it. More compact models suitable for small urban gardens are available, and while the contents may take longer to decompose, they will do so after a year or so, given a good mix of materials. If you have a densely planted garden and want to speed things up to make room in a small bin for more prunings and waste, try turning over the contents regularly to inject more air and bring the cool uncomposted outer layers into the warmer area in the centre. However, a small bin will never be as efficient as a large model, so buy or make the biggest one you can fit into your space.

> **TOP TIP** IF YOU ONLY HAVE SPACE FOR A SMALL BIN, WRAP SOME RECYCLED BUBBLE-PLASTIC PACKAGING OR AN OLD RUG OR CARPET AROUND THE EXTERIOR TO MAINTAIN HIGHER TEMPERATURES, ESPECIALLY IN WINTER.

Choose the largest bin you can fit into your space if you want to make compost quickly and efficiently.

Wooden boxes divided in half offer the same advantages as two bins but take up less space.

ONE BIN OR TWO?

In an ideal situation, you would have at least two bins and keen gardeners with big plots may even have three. Two large bins allow you to make a "hot heap", which has to be filled in one go and left to decompose (see pp.54–55), while accumulating waste material in the other, ready to make another hot heap when the first is finished. A third bin can be used as a holding area for matured compost. However, for people with small gardens, one bin will usually have to suffice and while it will make compost, you will probably have a layer of finished material at the bottom and raw waste on top. Some bins feature a hatch at the bottom that allows you to remove the finished compost more easily (see p.44).

THE COVER UP

Whether you have a bin or open heap, it is important to cover the composting materials. A lid or waterproof cover will prevent rain from washing away the nutrients, as well as ensuring that large numbers of weed seeds do not float in and settle on the compost. However, covers can cause the contents to dry out quickly, so the best advice is to partly cover all bins for the best of both worlds.

An old carpet will help to keep the rain out and retain the nutrients in an open-topped heap.

BUYING A BIN

There are many styles of bin on the market and the choice you make will depend on a number of factors, including the size of your garden, so weigh up the pros and cons to ensure a bin ticks all your boxes. Decorative wooden models can create an attractive focal point in a garden where a heap cannot be hidden from view, while tumbler bins that can make compost in just a few weeks may be the right choice if you have a small garden and lots of waste to process. The cost of bins varies greatly, too, so check what you are getting for your money and remember that big is usually best.

MAKING YOUR CHOICE

When selecting a bin, factors to consider before making your final decision will probably include the price, style, durability, and size. A plain black plastic conical model will usually be the cheapest option, or may even be free from your local authority. This type of basic bin would be suitable if you can place it where it will not create an eyesore, such as behind a shed, although hiding it out of sight may also mean it is less accessible (for more on siting your bin, see pp.52–53). To reduce the plastic pollution in the environment, opt for a bin made from recycled materials.

Prettier models, such as beehive-style bins, are often made from biodegradable wood, but also check that they have Forest Stewardship Council (FSC) certification showing that the timber is from a renewable source. Some are quite small, and will therefore need careful management and take longer to produce compost.

Other bins, such as the Johanna bin and tumbler types, may claim to speed up the composting process, but consider how easy they are to use before rushing into a purchase. Some tumblers, for example, are rolled along the ground, which requires strength and could potentially strain your back.

Bins with a hatch at the bottom allow easier access to the finished compost.

EASY ACCESS

Look for a bin with a wide top that allows you to fill it easily, and also bear in mind how you will access the finished compost. In the case of a plastic conical model that does not have a hatch or tray at the bottom, this will mean lifting off the bin and placing it close by, removing the compost and refilling the empty bin with any undecomposed material. Some wooden models have removable slats on one side, allowing you to add more as you fill up the bin, and take them out to get to the finished compost. If buying a bin with a fixed frame, think about how you will remove the heavy compost when it is ready.

If you want a plastic bin, select one made from recycled materials to lower your carbon footprint.

PROS AND CONS OF BOUGHT BINS

CONICAL PLASTIC BIN

PROS Inexpensive and practical. Models come in a wide range of sizes. Some types are made from more eco-friendly recycled plastic.
CONS Not very attractive. Contents may need turning to inject more air. Plastic units do not retain heat as well as wooden models. Removing the finished compost requires space and strength to lift off the bin. Made from non-biodegradable materials.

BIN WITH HATCH

PROS Can be inexpensive, depending on the design. Allows you to access finished compost while still filling up the top. Some models are made from eco-friendly recycled plastic or FSC-certified wood.
CONS After removing the compost you may need to push the other ingredients down to fill the void. The hatches or hinges can break, although replacements are sometimes available. May bring non-biodegradable material into the garden.

BEEHIVE-STYLE BIN

PROS Attractive in a small garden setting. Some models are made from FSC-certified, biodegradable wood (check with manufacturer). Hinged lid and large opening offers easy access. A wooden drawer or hatch allows easy removal of finished compost.
CONS Usually expensive. Few are large enough for quick composting methods (*see pp.54–55*). Models painted in pale colours will not heat up as quickly as darker-coloured wood or plastic.

TUMBLER BIN

PROS Manufacturers claim this type makes compost quicker than static models, although some studies show that large hot heaps are just as fast. Can reach high temperatures that kill weeds and pathogens. Eliminates problems with vermin.
CONS Expensive. Fast compost requires regular turning. Some tumblers need space to roll them and this will take effort too. Excludes worms, which help to kill weed seeds and increase

the nutrient content of the compost. Not very well insulated. The finished compost often has a coarse texture.

STACKABLE BIN

PROS Often made from biodegradable wood. The layers make access easy; you add a new stack as you fill up the bin. You may find inexpensive kits that you put together yourself.
CONS Space needed to store unused stacks. Some models are made from non-biodegradable plastic.

JOHANNA BIN

PROS Can compost cooked food, including fish, meat, bones, and dairy. Perforated base allows decomposers in, but keeps vermin out. Good for hot composting method (*see pp.54–55*). A hatch allows access to mature compost.
CONS Expensive, although some local authorities may offer a discount. Requires frequent stirring or turning for fast results. The insulating jacket for the bin is made from non-biodegradable foam polyethylene.

Beehive-style bin

Tumbler bin

Johanna bin

HOMEMADE HEAPS

One of the reasons many gardeners want to recycle their food and garden waste is to lower their carbon footprint and contribute to the welfare of the planet. Buying a manufactured bin is a practical solution for many, but creating your own from recycled materials reduces the pollution that industry and transportation generate. Plastic is especially polluting, both during its manufacture and when it goes to landfill. Homemade compost bins can be easy to construct, and some may take less time to put together than a trip to your DIY store or garden centre.

Straight stems from a pollarded or coppiced tree can be woven together tightly to create a beautiful bin.

Builders' bags can be transformed into practical compost bins within minutes.

EASY BIN BAGS

The ideal compost heap measures 1 cubic metre (1 cubic yard), which is about the same size as the average builders' bag of gravel or soil that you or your neighbours may have had delivered for use in the garden. The bags are made from durable cotton or manmade fabric and the only alteration required to transform them into a compost bin is to cut out a large square from the base so the decomposer minibeasts can find their way in. Remember to also partly cover the composting material to help insulate the contents.

TIMBER CONSTRUCTIONS

One of the easiest ways to make a wooden bin is with pallets (see pp.50–51), which are widely available from garden centres, DIY stores, and online. Alternatively, you could construct a more attractive bin from timber boards, screwed together with wood offcuts, to create four walls, with the gaps between each board no wider than 2.5cm (1in). The bin will then provide good insulation and prevent too much air from flowing through and cooling down or drying out the contents. Attach the four walls using stainless-steel screws and wooden corner blocks or metal joining plates. Old wooden floorboards, scaffold boards or fencing panels would be ideal materials for such a bin; other options include house doors or kitchen cabinets, if you can find some that are roughly the same size (or can be cut down to fit).

Source wooden items from salvage yards and freecycle websites, but make sure that the timber has not been treated with toxic chemicals such as creosote, which are hazardous to health.

Old wooden floorboards can be reused to construct a smart bin in the garden.

HEAPS OF HAY

Transforming a few bales of hay (or straw) into a practical compost heap is an inexpensive yet effective choice for a large garden or allotment. Hay bales offer excellent insulation, while allowing enough air in to create ideal conditions for the decomposers. Before buying, check that the hay is from an organic farm and it has been grown without the use of pesticides and herbicides, which may leach into your compost and kill your decomposers and plants.

To make the bin, simply set the hay bales in a square or rectangular shape to form three or four sides, staggering them like a brick wall for stability if you are creating a multi-layer structure. You can also knock in some wooden posts around the outer edges to keep the bales in place. Once the heap is filled, partly cover the contents with a waterproof material. The hay will gradually decompose, along with the contents, but the walls should remain intact for a year or so. You can then mix the decomposing hay into a new bin, constructed in the same way.

Bales of hay retain heat and help to speed up the composting process.

| **TOP TIP** HAY BALES CAN BE VERY HEAVY, SO ASK A FRIEND TO HELP YOU MOVE THEM INTO PLACE TO PREVENT INJURY.

OTHER OPTIONS

Be inventive when thinking of materials that could be used to create your compost bin. Try weaving together the straight stems cut from pollarded or coppiced trees in your garden, which will make a beautiful bin that will not need to be hidden from view. If you do not have straight stems, use a mallet to knock large, irregular-sized prunings into the ground to form a semi-circle and line the structure with corrugated card for extra insulation.

Old paving slabs or bricks can also be used to construct a box, or you can repurpose an old dustbin. To transform a plastic dustbin, use a sharp knife, hand saw, or jigsaw to cut out a large hole in the bottom that will allow minibeasts to enter and moisture to drain out.

You can use any non-toxic recycled materials, including old concrete slabs that may otherwise go to landfill.

THE HEAT IS ON

If there are large gaps in your homemade bin due to the materials used, insulate it by lining the structure with layers of corrugated cardboard, other paper packaging material, or old woollen clothing. The biodegradable materials will gradually decompose but more slowly than the other contents of your bin. You can also use wooden offcuts to cover up any holes or gaps, or try wrapping the outside of a bin with reused bubble plastic packaging. Do not add plastic to the inside edges of the bin, as it may harm the decomposers and pollute your finished compost.

AN EASY BIN FOR BEGINNERS

You do not need any previous DIY skills to make this simple chicken wire and cardboard bin. If you want to be really eco-friendly, try to source used materials from friends and neighbours, salvage yards, and freecycle websites. The bin also makes excellent use of the cardboard packaging you may have at home, and has an even lower carbon footprint than sending it for kerbside recycling, which entails transportation and processing. The whole project should not take more than a couple of hours to create.

FIRST THINGS FIRST

The wooden posts and chicken wire used for the main structure of this compost bin will last for many years and may be difficult to move, so find a good location for it before you start building (see pp.52–53).

Decide how wide and tall you want your bin to be – this heap is for a large garden that produces plenty of waste to fill it, but you can simply buy shorter wooden posts and make a smaller structure to fit your space. When using recycled materials, check that the wood is from an FSC certified source and has not been treated with toxic chemicals such as creosote. You could use sturdy tree prunings instead of buying wood – ask a local tree surgeon if they can spare some if you do not have a tree. If you are new to DIY, you may also be able to save money by borrowing the tools needed for the job from friends or neighbours.

> **TOP TIP** IF MAKING A SHORTER BIN, YOU CAN ADD A FOURTH SIDE TO THIS CONSTRUCTION AND FILL IT FROM THE TOP. THIS WOULD PROVIDE EXTRA INSULATION WHICH MAY SPEED UP THE COMPOSTING PROCESS.

Homemade bins can produce nutrient-rich, crumbly compost within a few months if they are large enough and situated in a sheltered spot.

YOU WILL NEED String and pegs •
Rubber mallet • 4 wooden posts (those
used here are 1.5m/5ft long) • Chicken
wire, approx. 1.2 × 2.5m (4 × 8ft) •
Fencing staples • Hammer and wire
cutters • Cardboard box packaging •
Waterproof material for cover

1 Measure out the size of the bin you
  want to create with string and pegs;
  this one is about 75cm (2½ft) square.
  Using the mallet, drive each post
  about 30cm (12in) into the ground at
  the corners. Wrap the chicken wire
  around the posts, cutting it to size
  if necessary.

2 Secure the chicken wire to the posts
  by hammering in fencing staples
  at three or four points along their
  length. Snip off any excess wire using
  wire cutters, making sure there are
  no sharp edges that may cause injury.
  If making a tall bin such as this, leave
  one side open to allow you to fill it.

3 Flatten your cardboard and use it to
  line the inside of the structure. To
  keep it in place, have some composting
  material to hand and add a layer of
  twigs to the base, then more green
  and brown waste on top (see
  pp.32–33). You may need to staple
  the top sections to the posts.

4 Keep filling up the bin as you
  accumulate garden and kitchen
  waste, layering it as described in
  the method you wish to use (see
  pp.54–61). The large size of this
  bin would lend itself to fast hot
  composting if you had enough
  material to fill it up in one go.

5 If you accumulate a large quantity of
  green waste such as grass clippings,
  make sure you include it in thin layers
  or add plenty of brown waste such
  as shredded prunings, cardboard, and
  scrunched paper to balance it out.

6 Each time you add to the heap,
  remember to partly cover the
  contents using an insulating material
  such as an old rug or plastic sheet.

MAKING A BIN FROM PALLETS

The pallets used by many industries for transporting goods are relatively easy to screw together to create a practical compost bin. However, you will need some expertise to make this more sophisticated model, which features a hinged door at the base that allows you to remove the finished compost without taking out all of the contents. DIY novices may wish to leave out this feature and make a simple four-sided bin instead. The inside of the bin can also be insulated with a layer or two of thick cardboard or natural cloth, which will help to speed up the composting process.

CHOOSING WOODEN PALLETS

Pallets are widely available and often come with home deliveries of building materials or garden soil and aggregates. You may also find them free of charge on local freecycling websites, or ask your local DIY store or garden centre if they have any that you can use. Before acquiring any pallets for a compost bin, check them for an IPPC or EPAL logo. These certifications show that the wood has not been treated with toxic chemicals. Reject any pallets displaying the letters MB, which indicates that they have been treated with a pesticide called methyl bromide that will harm the compost decomposers. If the pallets have no logos, they were probably used for domestic transportation and will not have been treated with chemicals.

NEED TO KNOW
- Pallets are made from softwood. This will decay after a while, especially when filled with wet compost. Check the structure annually, and if it is too weak, build a replacement.
- Do not paint your pallet bin with wood preservatives, which may harm the decomposers and pollute the finished compost.

Recycled wooden pallets make sturdy compost bins that last for some years.

TOP TIP PALLETS SHOULD STAND UP ON THEIR OWN ON REASONABLY LEVEL GROUND, BUT IT IS SAFER TO ASK A FRIEND TO HELP YOU HOLD THEM IN POSITION DURING CONSTRUCTION, ESPECIALLY IN WINDY CONDITIONS WHEN THEY MAY BLOW OVER.

HOW TO MAKE THE BIN

YOU WILL NEED 4 pallets of about the same size • Handsaw • Manual or power screwdriver • Stainless steel heavy-gauge screws • Wood offcuts • G-clamp (optional) • 2 heavy-duty gate hinges

1 Locate your bin on level ground, adding or removing soil if need be to ensure the structure will be stable. Position four pallets to create the sides of a square. If including a hinged hatch, cut about one-third off the bottom of one pallet and put that section aside before screwing the remaining section to the other sides, leaving a gap at the bottom.

2 Using a screwdriver, drive two or three heavy-gauge screws into the solid wooden sections of the pallets at each corner, top and bottom. Make sure that the pallets line up neatly.

3 Strengthen the joints by screwing offcuts of timber to the pallets where required. You may need to use a G-clamp to secure the wood while you screw it into place. Aim to create a sturdy structure that will withstand the weight of a large volume of heavy green and brown waste pressing against the sides.

4 If creating a bin with a hatch, position the section of pallet you put to one side in Step 1 so that it butts up to the section that you fixed to the main bin. Use a clamp or ask a friend to keep it place while you attach it.

5 Fix a pair of heavy-duty gate hinges to both sections, as shown, making sure that the access hatch opens and closes easily. To hold it shut, use a hammer to drive a stake into the ground or place bricks or large stones in front of it.

6 Finally, make a rudimentary catch to hold the hatch open when the compost is being removed. Use a single screw to attach a short piece of wood, but do not tighten it up completely so the catch can swivel and keep the open hatch in place.

SITING A HEAP OR BIN

There are a number of key factors to bear in mind when locating a heap or bin. Warmth will speed up the rate at which compost is produced, but in a small garden, siting your bin in a sunny spot that would otherwise be used for an attractive plant display may not be your best option. Also consider the appearance of your bin: unless it is a decorative model, position it carefully so that it is not an unintentional focal point from the house or patio. Keep your bin away from seating areas, too, which may be affected by the musty smell produced by fresh waste as it starts to decompose.

In a small garden where a utilitarian bin cannot be hidden easily, disguise it behind a bed of flowers.

Setting up a bin or two close to a paved path makes them easier to access with a wheelbarrow when the ground is wet.

ROUTE TO SUCCESS

When siting your bin, consider how you will access it with a barrowful of garden waste or scraps from the kitchen. Positioning it close to a pathway with a hard surface will make it easier to reach in wet weather, and will prevent a heavy wheelbarrow compacting the soil.

Avoid setting a compost bin on the far side of a lawn if you will need to use a route across the grass to reach it, as you may unwittingly create a muddy path of worn turf in the process. Choose a spot close enough to the kitchen to allow frequent trips to and fro, but not so close that you can smell any odours the compost produces from your back door. Remember to allow sufficient space around the bin to turn the contents, if you choose to do so. In a small garden, where it is difficult to hide your compost, opt for a decorative wooden bin or disguise it with a frill of flowers or shrubs.

SUN VS SHADE

The optimum position for your bin will be an area that is sheltered from the prevailing winds and receives sun for a few hours each day. This will provide the right heat to keep the decomposers happy. If you do not have the ideal spot, you can also set up your bin in shade, but remember that the cooler conditions will slow down the composting process, so you will need to be patient and wait a little longer for your black gold to form. Placing a heap in full sun is not recommended because the contents will dry out too quickly, which will kill some decomposers and encourage others to move out.

Composting will be quicker in a bin warmed by the sun for some of the day.

TOP TIP SOME PERNICIOUS WEEDS SUCH AS BINDWEED (*CALYSTEGIA SEPIUM*) OR HORSETAIL (*EQUISETUM ARVENSE*) WILL SURVIVE LIFE IN A COOL COMPOST HEAP, SO CHECK THAT THERE ARE NO TRACES OF THEM IN THE GROUND WHERE YOU PLAN TO SET UP YOUR BIN OR HEAP.

Install your compost heap on bare ground so that the decomposers in the soil can find their way inside.

SOFT LANDING

Place your bin on bare soil so that the decomposers can make their way into it and excess moisture can drain directly into the ground. If you have a bin with closed sides and a fitted lid, you can prevent vermin accessing the contents from below by lining the base with wire mesh. To do this, dig a shallow hole about 2.5cm (1in) deep and a little larger than the base of your bin. Line it with mesh cut to size and then place the bin on top. Vermin will be able to get into open-topped heaps or those with slatted sides, but you can deter them by not including cooked food, meat, or fish (see pp.32–35).

On a terrace or in a paved courtyard garden, remove the paving stones in the area where you are proposing to install your bin, or place it on top of a raised bed filled with soil. Setting a bin directly on a hard surface is possible, but the contents will stain the paving and you will need to add a shovelful of garden soil or mature homemade compost to introduce the decomposers. Also make sure the liquid that seeps out of it won't run off into a pond, where it will pollute the water.

BOLSTER YOUR BEDS

The area directly under a compost heap is incredibly fertile and will boost the productivity of the soil in garden beds and on allotments planted with hungry crops such as leafy greens. If you have space, place a bin or heap directly on a spare bed for a year or so and leave the contents to rot down, allowing the nutrient-rich liquid they produce to seep into the soil where it is needed. The finished compost can also be spread over the bed as a mulch before you plant it up with the next season's crops. You can then move the bin to another bed that needs enriching.

Two plastic bins are being used here to enrich the soil on a productive bed.

TRADITIONAL HOT COMPOSTING

The high temperatures achieved by hot composting can kill weeds and plant pathogens, and may produce crumbly compost in just a few weeks. This method is only viable for those with large gardens and a lot of waste, and it requires time, energy, and strength to turn the heap regularly. It will not work in small bins, where the volume of food is insufficient for the decomposers to generate enough heat.

Allotment holders can pool their waste materials to create one large heap for quick hot composting.

Large, well-insulated bins are needed for successful hot composting.

THE HEAT IS ON

This traditional method of composting requires a large heap of at least 1 cubic metre (1 cubic yard), or with a 1000 litre (227 US gallon) capacity. It is a quick and efficient method for anyone with a big garden or allotment who can accumulate sufficient garden waste and kitchen scraps to fill the bin all in one go. One of the main benefits of a traditional hot compost heap is that heat generated by the bacteria as they work on the plentiful food supply can kill most weeds and plant diseases. Temperatures of up to 60–70°C (140–158°F) also deliver crumbly compost in just a few weeks. However, if you have only a small garden or do not have the time or inclination to turn over a large bin full of composting ingredients every few days (see *opposite*), you can try easier methods instead, such as cool composting (see *pp.56–57*) or the high-fibre method (see *pp.60–61*).

FILLING A HOT HEAP

To create the ideal conditions for a hot compost heap, you will need to accumulate a good balance of green and brown waste (see pp.32–35) – a 2:1 ratio of green to brown materials or equal amounts of each is best.

To ensure the process works well, it is best to shred woody matter, such as tree branches and shrub stems, to give the fungi decomposers a greater surface area to work on. If you do not own a shredder, collect together your woody prunings throughout the year in a quiet corner of the garden and hire a machine for a day or two to process them.

Mix your greens and browns together before adding them to the heap, ensuring grass clippings and other soft green waste are blended well with scrunched-up paper and cardboard and shredded prunings so that they do not fall to the bottom and create a wet, airless mass. As you fill your bin, water the ingredients if they are dry and add a small bucket of garden soil or mature compost to introduce plenty of decomposers into the mix. A few layers of rotted animal manure will also help to inject nitrogen and ensure the bacteria work fast to produce those high temperatures. A waterproof cover laid partially over the top will help to insulate the contents and prevent nutrients from washing away in the rain.

> **TOP TIP** WITH TWO BINS, YOU CAN MAKE A HOT HEAP IN ONE WHILE ACCUMULATING WASTE IN THE SECOND, READY TO FILL THE FIRST AFTER THE FINISHED COMPOST IS REMOVED.

Mix your green and brown compost ingredients together well before you add them to a hot heap.

TURNING THE CONTENTS

Once the bin is full, the mesophilic bacteria will get to work and the ingredients will heat up within a few days (see pp.20–21). When you remove the cover from the bin, the contents will feel warm, and they will be hotter in the centre. You can install a metal stake into the middle of the bin to gauge the heat. After about a week, the food supply and oxygen in the bin will start to run out and the composting material will cool down. At this point, remove all the contents and mix them up again, so that uncomposted material on the cooler edges is in the centre of the bin when you refill it. Alternatively, use a fork to bring uncomposted ingredients into the centre of the heap. Water the contents if they are dry. Turning the compost in this way introduces more air and undigested food for the decomposers to get to work on once more, and the bin will heat up again. Continue to mix up the ingredients every few days until the compost does not heat up any more. Then leave it to mature for a month or two, depending on the season – the process will take longer in cold weather.

Turning the contents of your heap brings uncomposted ingredients into the centre and injects more air into it.

NEED TO KNOW

- Set up a hot compost bin in a warm, sheltered area – cold locations will prevent the contents from heating up sufficiently.
- Insulate slatted wooden bins by lining the inner edges with cardboard or woollen materials.
- Import well-rotted animal manures to increase the nitrogen content that the decomposers require.
- Regularly check that the contents of the bin have not dried out. If they have, either water them or remove the cover if rain is forecast.

COMPOSTING THE COOL WAY

There are alternatives to the hot composting method (see pp.54–55) if you have a small garden and not enough waste to make a bin heat up. "Slow stack" or "cool composting" allows you to produce compost in a smaller bin and it will form a crumbly mix if you can wait a year or more for the final product. This method also allows you to fill your bin gradually as ingredients become available.

Start your cool heap or bin with enough green and brown materials for a layer 30cm (12in) deep.

Cool composting works well in gardens where there is only space for a medium-sized or small bin.

DIVIDING YOUR WASTE

Many gardeners find that they can maintain a constant stream of green waste from the kitchen and garden, but have a seasonal glut of brown waste at pruning time during late winter and spring. A solution is to stockpile your brown waste, which will take a long time to decompose on its own, in a separate bin or a quiet area of the garden. You can then include it in layers when it is needed to balance your green materials. Shred large branches and stems, which will not compost down, before adding them to your bin.

Gluts of green waste can be more problematic since it decomposes into airless sludge within a week or two. If you have too many greens, consider the high fibre method (pp.60–61) or try trench composting (pp.62–63).

HOW COOL HEAPS WORK

The principles of the cool compost method mirror the processes that take place in a woodland (see pp.14–15), where dead plant material builds up over time and gradually decomposes, but never heats up to the levels of a hot heap. The decomposer communities, including minibeasts and mesophilic microorganisms, that work in cooler conditions (see pp.20–21) break down the waste matter you throw in, but the process takes a lot longer than in a hot heap. However, be patient and you will find the same finished product in your bin after a year or so, ready to use in the garden. Remember that cool methods do not reach the temperatures required to kill off plant pathogens or weed seeds, including those of pernicious weeds, so do not include these in your heap or bin.

Store spare prunings in an old dustbin for use later in the year.

FILLING A COOL BIN

To start the process of cool composting, collect green and brown waste from the materials described on pp.32–33, such as kitchen scraps, cardboard, twiggy prunings, and leaves, to create a depth in the bin of 30cm (12in) or more. Spread a layer of twigs at the bottom of the bin to help increase the airflow from the base. Then start filling by alternating layers of green and brown materials, spreading them evenly, right up to the edges of the bin. Use a rake to push down the ingredients, while ensuring that you do not remove all of the air gaps. Water every 30–60cm (12–24in), unless your waste is already wet.

Add ingredients to the bin as they become available, but try to include as much as possible in batches. For example, use a caddy in the kitchen to collect a few days' worth of scraps before adding them together with brown waste such as egg cartons or scrunched-up cardboard, plus some shredded woody waste.

The bin may never fill up completely since the waste will reduce in volume as it rots down. At some point, you can decide to stop adding to it and leave all the ingredients to complete the composting process – this may take a few months or a year in cold weather conditions. Alternatively, you can continue to fill the bin and after about a year remove all the ingredients, placing any uncomposted material to one side while you take out the dark, crumbly, sweet-smelling material at the bottom. You can then use the uncomposted material to refill the empty bin, adding it on top of a layer of twigs to start the process off again.

> **TOP TIP** WHEN MOST OF YOUR COMPOST IS FINISHED IT MAY STILL CONTAIN RECOGNIZABLE TWIGS, CORN COBS AND OTHER WOODY ITEMS. TO REMOVE THEM, COVER YOUR WHEELBARROW WITH CHICKEN WIRE AND FORK THE MIX INTO IT. THIS TRAPS LARGE ITEMS THAT CAN THEN BE RETURNED WHOLE, OR CUT UP INTO SMALLER SECTIONS, TO THE BIN FOR FURTHER COMPOSTING.

The lid keeps out rain and insulates the bin

Alternate layers of green and brown material

Add autumn leaves in thin layers or compost them separately

Put a layer of twiggy brown prunings at the bottom to aid air flow

Layering green and brown materials promotes a good structure and results in dark, sweet-smelling compost to use on the garden.

Wear gloves when adding fresh or pelleted poultry manure to activate a sluggish compost bin.

COMPOST ACTIVATORS

If your bin seems to have ground to a halt and the material is not composting down, try turning over or mixing up the contents, as described for hot composting (see p.55). To activate it further, you can also inject it with a high dose of nitrogren by adding a thin layer of poultry manure (see p.36) and watering it in, or pouring a small bucket of human urine over the ingredients every day for a week or two – the latter is safe to use as long as you are healthy, do not have an infection or disease, and are not taking medication. Collecting some garden worms, which come to the surface after rain, and adding them to the pile will also help to speed up a cool heap, or you can purchase a compost activator from the garden centre, which should also motivate your decomposers.

COMPOSTING PROBLEM-SOLVER

There are many reasons why a hot or cool compost method may not be working as well as it should do. The problems are usually relatively easy to fix, especially when you understand how the process works and the conditions the decomposers require to function well. One concern beginners often have is that the final product does not look like potting medium you buy in the shops, but this is not a problem. Homemade compost is usually coarser in texture, unless you can wait a few years for it to break down further, but it will still make an excellent soil conditioner and slow-release plant food.

WHY PROBLEMS ARISE

Composting often slows down or halts altogether because the decomposers run out of food or air, in which case they move out of the bin, become spores and wait for conditions to improve, or die. These problems can be solved by turning the contents, adding more food, and increasing the brown materials in the bin. Other problems are equally easy to tackle once you know what is wrong.

TOO COLD? Small bins or those with large gaps in the sides often allow too much heat to escape, which slows down the composting process. Try relocating your bin to a warmer, sheltered spot and wrapping the outside of the structure in bubble plastic or similar waterproof insulating material in winter to help to keep the heat in. Lining wooden bins with layers of thick card, hay, or pieces of wood to block the gaps may help too.

TOO HOT? Very occasionally large municipal heaps may spontaneously combust during dry weather when temperatures exceed 120°C (248°F), but this is rarely a problem for gardeners. Only a heap of more than 2 sq m (22 sq ft) runs a slight risk of catching on fire, but most will never reach more than 70°C (158°F) before cooling down. Keeping the ingredients well-watered reduces this risk further.

TOO WET? One of the most common problems for gardeners is a bin that is too wet and has therefore become airless. One of the first signs is the smell of rotten eggs, which indicates that

Only huge heaps ever reach temperatures that could become too hot in summer.

anaerobic composting is taking place. The solution is to add brown waste to mop up the moisture and introduce more air, and to cover your bin if it is open to the elements. Lack of drainage at the bottom of the bin can also cause a wet heap. Mix in scrunched-up paper and cardboard, shredded wood, and small twigs until the bin no longer smells.

TOO DRY? Decomposers need moisture to keep them healthy, but bins and heaps often dry out in hot weather when evaporation rates are high, and when the brown ingredients outweigh greens. A tight-fitting lid can exacerbate the problem too, as it does not allow any rain to reach the contents. However, the problem is easily fixed by adding some more green waste, such as kitchen peelings and grass clippings, and, if necessary, watering the heap.

A heap or bin can become wet and airless if you add too many greens.

Air flow through gaps in a bin such as this will slow the decomposition process.

Vegetable waste from the garden or kitchen will increase moisture levels in an unproductive dry bin.

THE HIGH-FIBRE METHOD

Owners of small gardens often generate insufficient carbon-rich natural materials to balance the nitrogen-rich greens produced in the kitchen. A simple way to solve this problem is to use the large volumes of paper and card waste that many households accumulate. The experts have dubbed this the "high-fibre" method because the paper performs a similar digestive function as fibrous foods do in our own diet.

The high-fibre method uses assorted waste from the kitchen.

HIGH-FIBRE ESSENTIALS

The high-fibre method of composting is good for owners of small gardens without space for a large hot compost bin, and for people using the conical models available from local councils. However, it will work best in a bin with a capacity of 300 litres (68 US gallons) or more, so buy or make the largest model you can fit into your garden.

Working in a similar way to cool composting (see pp.56–57), this method produces compost slowly and the contents of the bin will not heat up sufficiently to kill weeds and plant pathogens, so make sure you do not add these to the mix. It replaces carbon-rich materials from the garden, such as twigs, shredded wood, and leaves, with cardboard and other paper products. These are needed to create the "bread" in the compost sandwich (see p.26) and provide energy for the decomposers, while also maintaining a good structure to keep the bin aerated. A deficiency of browns leads to a soupy, airless mix that will smell and emit toxic gases that pollute the atmosphere (see p.30).

Use the high-fibre method if your garden does not produce much carbon-rich woody waste throughout the year.

HOW TO FILL YOUR BIN

As well as collecting your green kitchen waste, put to one side cardboard packaging and paper products (*see right*), removing any tape and staples before you do so. You can store these greens and browns separately or mix them up, but make sure the paper and card is scrunched-up before adding it to your bin. Tear larger items such as boxes into irregular-shaped pieces, if you cannot scrunch them up easily, but do not flatten them, as this will squeeze out the air. As a guide, try to create fist-sized balls, though the pieces can be slightly smaller or larger without creating a problem.

To start off your bin, put a 20–30cm (8–12in) layer of scrunched-up paper and card in the bottom, together with a couple of spadefuls of homemade compost or garden soil to populate the contents with decomposers. Worms are particularly useful for this method, so collect a few after it has rained and they have surfaced in the garden. If you cannot find any worms, buy them from fishing-tackle or wormery suppliers. Then simply top up the bin with the soft green waste from the kitchen and garden. If you want to add grass clippings, limit them to layers of no deeper than 15cm (6in), or add more paper and card if you have a larger amount. You can add layers of twigs too, but include more greens if you notice composting slowing down or stopping.

Eggboxes do not need to be scrunched-up because they already contain plenty of air.

REMOVING THE COMPOST

The high-fibre method will take up to a year to produce crumbly, sweet-smelling compost, which you can harvest from the bottom of the bin. If you are adding to the bin regularly, you will also have an uncomposted layer at the top, which you can either remove and fork into a second bin, if you have one, or put to one side while you take out the composted material. Also remove the worm-rich layer just below it and add to a second bin or set it aside along with the uncomposted items. You can then fill the empty bin with card, paper, and compost, as described above, adding the uncomposted and worm-rich material on top.

When removing the compost, take out the worm-rich layer just below the surface to start the process again.

TRENCH COMPOSTING

Burying nitrogen-rich food and garden waste in the ground is an effective way to recycle nutrients and revitalize infertile plots. You can also use this method to compost meat, fish, and dairy products, if you put them at the bottom of the trench so that the smell does not attract vermin. All you need is a spade and the strength to dig a large hole.

TRENCH BENEFITS

This form of composting improves the structure of the soil and makes nutrients available to plants' roots exactly where they are needed, such as on an allotment plot or in a vegetable garden where you plan to plant hungry crops. Trench composting offers a good way of recycling excess kitchen and garden waste that will not fit into your bin, or you can use it instead of creating a bin or heap if you do not have space for one in a small garden. Filling a long trench with waste is the most common technique, but you can also excavate a number of individual pits if you accumulate waste in smaller batches or have a limited area to plant up.

> **TOP TIP** USE A MARKER TO INDICATE WHERE YOU HAVE BURIED YOUR WASTE MATERIAL SO THAT YOU DO NOT DIG IT UP BY MISTAKE WHEN PLANTING.

Plant hungry crops, such as sweetcorn, into the enriched soil.

Cover your trench with at least 30cm (12in) of soil to ensure good insulation over winter and to disguise the smell.

CREATING A TRENCH

The best time for many gardeners to create a trench is in autumn, which allows time for the waste to decompose over winter and early spring and release its nutrients for annual crops or flowers planted later in the year. Trenches made at other times will need to be left fallow for a few months while the buried materials rot down.

Start by digging a trench 45–60cm (18–24in) deep, about the width of two spades, and the length you will need to bury your waste material. Pile up the excavated soil beside the trench. Fill the bottom with about 15cm (6in) of food and leafy garden waste, but do not add perennial weeds. If you removed grass turves to dig your trench, turn them upside down so the roots are facing up, and add these on top. Cover with at least 30–45cm (12–18in) of soil and tamp down with the back of a rake.

WAIT BEFORE PLANTING

The process of decomposition is faster in the ground in winter than it would be in an open heap, especially if you add an insulating mulch over your trench, but the waste will still take a few months to rot, or up to a year in cold, poorly drained soils. Remember to water the trench during prolonged dry spells since the microbes and minibeasts do not function well in arid conditions.

You will notice a slight drop in the soil level over the trench when the materials have decomposed, or if you made a mound over your waste, it will start to level off. At this point, you can plant into the soil with hungry crops such as cabbages, sweetcorn, beans, and squashes, or ornamental plants in a flower garden. All will benefit from the nutrients that have been released and the increased worm activity that improves the soil structure.

Bruised windfalls can be composted easily in a trench close to the parent tree, but leave a few on the surface for the birds.

NO-BIN COMPOSTING

"Sheet" or "lasagne" composting is a quick and easy method that involves layering brown and green materials directly on the soil surface to decompose *in situ*. It is completely free, requiring no bin or homemade structure, and makes use of old cardboard packaging or newspapers, plus all the garden and kitchen waste you can lay your hands on. You can try it on any productive or ornamental beds that need improving. The "lasagne" name refers not to the ingredients but the way in which they are assembled in layers on the ground.

Try lasagne composting in raised beds to improve the growing conditions for edibles such as salads and soft fruits.

Collect green and brown waste from the garden to pile up on the soil surface.

FRIABLE AND FERTILE

Lasagne composting has many advantages for the soil, leaving the structure intact like a mulch (see pp.90–95) while delivering nutrients directly to where they are needed as the materials slowly decompose. The method also excludes light beneath the layers, which suppresses weeds. It will kill grass, too, offering an alternative to digging up turves or using herbicides when converting a lawn into a new bed. It can also be used on fallow land that you plan to plant up later.

All you need for lasagne composting are the usual waste materials, card or newspaper, and a little patience. Then, after a few months, you can plant up the improved soil you have produced.

WHEN TO START

Autumn is generally considered to be the best time to start this form of composting. The crops on many productive beds will have been harvested by then, leaving the land fallow but vulnerable to the ravages of winter weather, while weed seeds will be lying in wait, ready to spring into action when warmer weather returns. Covering the ground at this time throws a protective blanket over the soil that reduces erosion and prevents weeds from germinating. Winter rains will also keep the composting materials damp, while the card or newspaper helps to prevent nutrients leaching away too quickly.

You can use this composting method in spring if you prefer, but remember that the soil will not be ready for planting up until the autumn.

TOP TIP SPREADING THE COMPOSTABLE MIX OVER A BED MAKES IT MORE PRONE TO DRYING OUT IN WARM WEATHER. CHECK IT REGULARLY AND WATER IF THE MATERIALS ON THE TOP FEEL DRY.

A layer of damp cardboard blocks the light, preventing weed seeds in the soil from germinating in spring.

HOW TO MAKE LASAGNE COMPOST

YOU WILL NEED Newspaper or cardboard • Finished compost or topsoil • Watering can • Green and brown waste from the garden and kitchen

1 Collect together enough newspaper or cardboard to cover the plot you want to improve, as well as sufficient kitchen and garden waste to make a few deep layers. Use newspaper eight sheets thick, or a single layer of cardboard.

2 If you are using this method to convert a lawn, add some compost or topsoil over the grass to introduce the beneficial decomposer microbes. On either a lawn or fallow land, lay newspaper sheets or cardboard over the bed so that they overlap to exclude all the light. Water the materials thoroughly.

3 Spread out your green and brown materials (see pp.32–33) on top of the cardboard or paper in layers of each colour, with greens about twice as deep as browns if shredded woody material is used, or equal amounts of greens and browns if not.

4 Your green and brown waste pile can be any thickness up to about 50 cm (20in) deep. Remember that it is made up of mostly air and water and will quickly reduce in height, forming a slightly raised area in just a few weeks.

5 Water your layers of compostable materials so that everything is damp. To keep the materials in place and introduce yet more microbes, cover them with a final layer of mature compost or topsoil.

6 The lasagne mix should rot down within a few months, so if you started in autumn it will be ready to plant up by spring. If the card has not decomposed completely, cut a hole in it to allow the roots of your plants to reach the soil below.

MAKING LEAFMOULD

Autumn leaves contain high levels of carbon and are decomposed primarily by fungi, which work more slowly than the bacteria that break down young green growth and kitchen scraps. You can add thin layers of leaves to your compost bin to balance the nitrogen-rich greens, but it is best to compost large volumes of deciduous tree leaves on their own. After a year or two, they make a crumbly material known as leafmould, which can be used as a mulch, soil conditioner, or ingredient for homemade potting and seed composts.

In autumn, a deciduous tree reabsorbs nutrients in its leaves before they fall, to sustain it through the winter.

Transforming leaves from your garden into a free soil conditioner is easy but requires patience.

FOLIAGE FACTS

During the spring and summer, leaves contain 80 per cent of the nutrients that deciduous trees and shrubs take up through their roots, but as autumn approaches, the plants reabsorb most of these chemicals. The dead leaves that fall are therefore low in nutrients but contain a high proportion of lignin, the fibrous material that makes up woody plants' cell structures. Lignin is very slow to decompose, but it supports many forms of fungi that feed on it, including mycorrhizal fungi that help plant roots to absorb nutrients (see p.15). When spread over the soil as a mulch, the rotted leaves populate the soil with these beneficial fungi while providing food for worms and other minibeasts.

Gather the leaves covering a lawn with a besom broom or rake.

COLLECTING LEAVES

Use autumn leaves that are covering the hard surfaces and lawns in your garden, but allow those on beds and borders to decompose *in situ*. To speed up decomposition, you can put your mower's blades on a high setting and run them over the leaves to shred them. Including grass clippings in the mix will also inject the finished leafmould with some nitrogen.

You should not take leaves from natural woodlands because they play a crucial role in the natural cycling of nutrients (*see pp.14–15*), but you may be able to collect them from parks; seek permission before removing them. Avoid leaves found on busy roadsides, which will be coated with pollutants.

Foliage with a high lignin content, such as that of oak, chestnut, and beech, will decompose more slowly than hazel, willow, and maple leaves with lower levels, but they will all make good compost in the end. Fruit tree foliage may harbour scabs, rusts, blights, and other fungal diseases, so many experts advise against using it. Instead, bag up the leaves and take them to the municipal dump for hot composting.

COMPOSTING LEAVES

On a calm day, collect your leaves together and simply stuff them into an old plastic potting or seed compost bag, a hessian sack, or, if you have a large volume, a recycled builders' bag. Using a sharp knife, make some holes in the sides of the plastic or canvas bags to allow air to enter, and water the leaves if they are dry. Put the bags or sacks in a quiet corner of the garden, fold the tops over and keep them sealed with a brick or large stone on top. Alternatively, you can make a larger, more permanent container with chicken wire fixed to sturdy wooden or metal posts; when it is full, cover the leaves with cloth held down with stones or an old rug to prevent them blowing away.

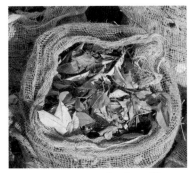

Hessian bags are perfect for making leafmould and can be added to the compost bin after they are no longer usable.

In a large garden, two chickenwire cages allow you to fill one while the leafmould in the other is maturing.

USING LEAFMOULD

After about one year, the leaves will have decomposed to produce a crumbly, rough-textured material that may contain visible shreds of foliage. This can be used as a mulch by spreading a 5cm (2in) layer over beds and borders, leaving a gap around the stems of woody plants. The mulch will protect the soil from winter rain which can wash out the nutrients. Worms will gradually take the leafmould down into the soil too, where fungi and, later, bacteria will continue to decompose it, releasing nutrients for plants to use. One-year-old leafmould also helps to aerate the soil, improves drainage, reduces weed growth, and makes a good topdressing for a lawn in autumn when it is applied sparingly over the grass.

If you have the patience to wait two years, the leaves will have transformed into a fine-textured material that can

Cover the soil in raised beds with a thick layer of leafmould to protect it over winter.

be used to make good-quality seed and potting composts for free (*see pp.96–97*). They will have a lower carbon footprint than products from a garden centre, too.

COMPOSTING PRUNINGS

An excess of woody waste can be a problem for gardeners because it may take more than two years to decompose in a compost bin. This is partly because large stems tend to dry out quickly, reducing decomposer activity, and partly because fungi, which tackle the wood, are slow workers. In the past, prunings were burned and the resulting potash-rich ash was used to feed the soil, but bonfires cause harmful air pollution and are now illegal in many areas. More eco-friendly methods include transforming prunings into a useful mulching material or stockpiling logs to make homes for wildlife.

A large hedge may produce too much woody waste to compost in a mixed bin.

RECYCLING WOODY WASTE

Twiggy tree and shrub prunings can provide the carbon-rich bread in the compost sandwich (see p.26), but because they take a long time to decompose you should only include them in thin layers. In addition, stems that are more than 2cm (¾in) in diameter will probably not compost down within a year, even in a hot heap, leaving you with large lumps in your black gold. This is because wood, like autumn leaves (see pp.66–67), has a high lignin content which fungi break down very slowly. Large branches also have a relatively small surface area for the microbes to work on; the best plan is to shred them, which creates more surfaces and helps to speed up the action. Woody stems and branches left intact allow large air gaps between them, too, which causes them to dry out and slows down decomposition.

SHRED AND MULCH

If you produce a glut of prunings in the winter or spring, or have hedges that generate large quantities of woody waste, consider hiring or buying a shredder to create wood chips. Prunings taken from living plants will contain nitrogen as well as carbon, and are the best sort to shred and add in thin layers to a bin – hot composting is an ideal way to use them. Alternatively, you can compost wood chips on their own in a tall, thin bin that uses the weight of the stacked material to compress it and remove large air gaps. Using this method, the wood chips will take at least two years to break down into coarse-textured compost, though adding activators such as urine will halve that time (see p.57). You can compost unshredded prunings, but only if you are prepared to wait three years.

Another way to use wood chips is to apply a 5–8cm (2–3in) layer of them over the soil to create a weed-suppressing mulch around fruit trees, or to make a naturalistic pathway through the garden or around vegetable beds.

> **TOP TIP** IF YOU DO NOT HAVE SUFFICIENT WOODY WASTE TO WARRANT HIRING A SHREDDER, ASK NEIGHBOURS IF YOU CAN POOL YOUR WASTE MATERIAL WITH THEIRS AND SHARE THE COST TO MAKE IT WORTHWHILE.

Use large quantities of shredded prunings to make a path around vegetable beds or through an informal garden.

HOMES FOR WILDLIFE

Large logs and thick stems cannot be shredded or composted easily, but they are still a valuable asset to the garden. Log piles make the perfect homes for many types of wildlife such as beetles and hibernating frogs and toads, which prey on insect plant pests and are a benefit to the gardener. Simply pile up your logs and branches in a quiet corner in partial shade, pushing twigs and leaves into the gaps. Avoid deep shade or full sun, which may be too cold or hot for minibeasts and other wildlife.

Stack spare logs and branches in a quiet area to create a wildlife habitat for minibeasts and hibernating amphibians.

THE HÜGELKULTUR METHOD

This method works on a similar principle to trench composting (see pp.62–63) but instead of burying your green waste you create mounds, known as hugels, of woody materials, green waste, and soil, which you then leave to decompose. This system of composting was described and named in the late 1970s by the German horticulturalists Hans Beba and Herman Andra, although there is historic evidence of its use hundreds of years earlier in Eastern Europe.

Start by digging a trench about 1.5m (5ft) wide and 30cm (12in) deep in a sunny area – it can be as long as you require. Set the soil to one side. Place logs and branches at the bottom of the trench and add a 20–30cm (8–12in) layer of nitrogen-rich greens, such as kitchen waste or grass clippings, along with smaller branches, twigs, wood chips, and leaves, to fill the gaps. You can also use any turf removed when digging the hole – turn it root-side up and place it over the logs before adding the nitrogen-rich greens and twiggy materials. Then apply a 10–15cm (4–6in) layer of semi-mature compost or manure. If you have sufficient

material, add another layer of slightly smaller logs and branches and infill as described above. Finally, cover the mound with the soil you initially excavated from the hole.

The decomposers will rot the contents and reduce the mound to half its height when the composting process is complete. This may take a year or more, but meanwhile you can plant into the soil covering the mound. Warmth generated by the decomposers speeds up growth, while the water-retentive areas on the sides of the mound and free drainage at the top suit many plants. As the mound rots down, it also delivers nutrients to the roots.

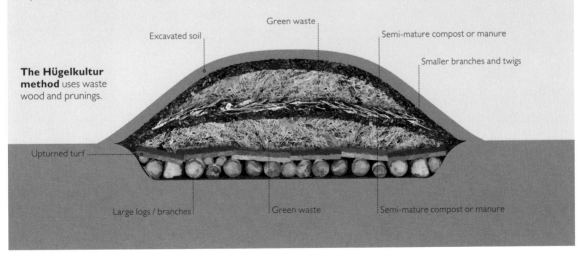

The Hügelkultur method uses waste wood and prunings.

Green waste

Excavated soil

Semi-mature compost or manure

Smaller branches and twigs

Upturned turf

Large logs / branches

Green waste

Semi-mature compost or manure

GRASSED UP

When composted in small quantities, lawn clippings deliver many benefits as they release plant nutrients, including nitrogen, potassium, and phosphorus, into the finished material. However, problems can arise when mowings are added in large quantities to a bin without sufficient carbon-rich absorbent materials to mop up the moisture they also produce. To make the best use of excess grass clippings, try a few different methods of composting and mulching, so that you keep them all in your garden rather than sending them out for recycling, and thus minimize your carbon footprint.

The clippings from a large lawn can be difficult to compost in an average-sized bin.

TOO GOOD BY HALF

People with lawns often accumulate large volumes of clippings each time they mow, which in the height of summer may be once a week or more. Grass is a very good source of nitrogen and has a C:N ratio of 20 (see pp.32–33). When included in a compost bin, lawn clippings help to accelerate the microbial activity, but add too many and you will soon find that your heap has deteriorated into a wet, airless soup, which will start to smell as the anaerobic decomposers move in (see p.30). Grass is made of 80–85 per cent water, which causes a problem when it is released by the microbes as they get to work on it – waterlogged conditions drive out the oxygen that decomposers need to survive. One solution is to leave the clippings on the lawn after mowing, rather than composting them (see pp.98–99). You can also add them to a mixed heap, applying the grass in thin layers, sandwiched between equal quantities of carbon-rich paper and card, hay, used potting compost, shredded leaves, or wood chips.

Large volumes of grass will create a wet, airless sludge in a compost bin unless you also add plenty of brown materials.

MAKING MULCHES FROM LAWN CLIPPINGS

A large lawn will produce too many clippings to add to the average-sized compost bin, but there are other ways to deal with an excess. You can leave them on the surface of the lawn for a few days during a spell of dry weather and then rake them up after midday, when any dew will have evaporated. Apply the dried grass in a 5cm (2in) layer as a mulch on your beds and borders, leaving a space around the stems of woody plants – deeper mulches may form a solid mat over the soil when wet, preventing oxygen and moisture from reaching plant roots. Grass mulches help to suppress weed growth, conserve moisture, and moderate soil temperatures. When taken down into the soil by worms they also release nutrients, especially nitrogen, for plants' roots to absorb.

Rake up dried grass clippings and apply them to beds and borders to form a weed-suppressing mulch.

TOP TIP DO NOT USE GRASS CLIPPINGS AS A MULCH OR IN YOUR COMPOST BIN IF THE LAWN HAS BEEN RECENTLY TREATED WITH A HERBICIDE, AS THESE PRODUCTS CAN HARM DECOMPOSERS AS WELL AS PLANTS.

Stack lawn turves grass-side down in a quiet corner to decompose into compost.

COMPOSTING TURF

When removing grass to make a new bed or border, you can chop up the turves into sections, checking first that they do not contain perennial weeds, and include them in your compost heap. If large turves are taking up too much space in your bin and slowing down the microbe activity, compost them separately instead. Turn them over so the grass is facing down, and stack them up evenly. Build your turf pile in a quiet corner of the garden or on a spare fruit or vegetable bed, where the resulting compost can be spread over the surface. The turves may rot down in six months in a sheltered location during spring and summer, but they could take up to year in colder sites or seasons.

GRASSBOARDING

Similar to the high-fibre technique of composting (see pp.60–61), grassboarding makes use of the paper and cardboard packaging materials you may have accumulated at home. It creates compost efficiently by sandwiching these brown carbon-rich materials with grass clippings, which have a high nitrogen content. Card packaging (particularly corrugated cardboard), egg cartons, newspaper, and used paper towels are ideal for this simple method. Rip up and scrunch the paper products, removing any plastic tape as you go, and put them into a large container with a hole in the bottom, a plastic compost bin, or a wooden bin on open soil in a sheltered spot. Tip in your lawn clippings so that they fall into the gaps between the paper and card, then continue to alternate the materials, using the grass in layers no deeper than 5cm (2in). Do not compress the paper materials, which provide air as well as carbon.

An alternative method, if you have a large volume of clippings, is to add the scrunched card as described above, then apply a 20cm (8in) layer of grass, followed by a 2–3cm (1in) layer of garden soil. Repeat these layers until the bin is full. Both of these methods will produce fine-textured, crumbly compost in 6–12 months.

Layer grass with card and paper materials to produce a fine-grade compost in 6–12 months.

PLANTING GREEN MANURES

Green manures are plants that store nutrients that they either absorb from the air, in the case of legumes, or from water in the soil through their deep roots. They release their goodness when composted, but rather than adding them to a bin you simply dig them into the ground where they are growing. You can sow green manures from spring to autumn, depending on how you wish to use them.

Green manures such as phacelia are composted directly in the ground where they have been growing.

WHY PLANT GREEN MANURES?

The plants that act as green manures have many benefits for the gardener. They increase soil fertility and improve its structure, increasing the moisture content of light sandy soils and the drainage in clays. Green manures belonging to the pea and bean family (legumes) are especially good for poor, infertile soils. They grow in a symbiotic relationship with bacteria that take nitrogen gas from the air in the soil and transfer this to nodules on the legumes' roots. When dug into the soil, these green manures release their nitrogen, which plants take up and use to produce healthy foliage (see pp.88–89).

The leafy canopies and dense roots of green manures also help to suppress weed growth and to protect soils from erosion during droughts and storms. In addition, many produce pollen- and nectar-rich flowers that attract beneficial insects such as bees and hoverflies; the latter also eat aphids and help to keep these pests at bay. The combined benefits of green manure plants create ideal growing conditions for many crops, and flowers too, if you are making a new ornamental garden.

Rake the bed to create a smooth surface before sowing your green manure crop.

PLANTING AND DIGGING IN

Choose a manure that will thrive in your soil and benefit the crops you plan to grow afterwards (see opposite). For example, try vetch over winter to stabilize soils and increase the nitrogen content for leafy crops sown afterwards. Fast-maturing crops such as phacelia or mustard are good choices for bare ground that may be overrun with weeds in between crop sowings, while black medick and fenugreek are ideal between slow-maturing crops such as sweetcorn.

When you have made your choices, prepare a bed by removing the weeds and lightly treading down the soil. Rake to create a smooth surface, then sow

Microbes and minibeasts decompose green manures dug into the soil.

the seeds, scattering them evenly. Large plants such as buckwheat and field beans are best planted in rows. Use a rake to cover the seed and water well.

Dig in plants three to four weeks before you want to sow or plant a crop, or as the green manure starts to mature and before it sets seed. Turn the plants over and cover them with soil, using a sharp spade to chop up clumps. Bury them no deeper than 15cm (6in) on heavy clay or 18cm (7in) on sandy soils. Alternatively, if you prefer not to dig the soil, leave spring- and summer-sown manures to die down over winter, or cover hardy plants with cardboard held down with stones, and leave the plants to rot in situ.

CHOOSING GREEN MANURES

This list of green manures and their benefits will help you to choose those that are right for your soil and crop choices.

GREEN MANURE	WHEN TO SOW	SOIL TYPE	GROWING TIME
Buckwheat (*Fagopyrum esculentum*) A fast-growing half-hardy annual, buckwheat will return phosphorous to the soil, which plants need for healthy roots and shoots. Its leaves also help to suppress weeds.	spring to midsummer	free-draining/infertile	1–3 months
Black medick (*Medicago lupulina*) A short hardy biennial plant, black medick is a good crop for growing between larger, slow-growing crops such as sweetcorn.	spring to midsummer	free-draining	3+ months
Alfalfa (*Medicago sativa*) The deep roots of this hardy perennial legume help to break up heavy clays. It will also recycle nitrogen from the air into a form that other plants can use.	late spring to midsummer	acid and poorly drained soils	12+ months
Phacelia (*Phacelia tanacetifolia*) Fast-growing, this half-hardy annual suppresses weeds, the flowers attract pollinators, and the plants return a range of nutrients to the soil for the next crop of plants to take up.	early spring to early autumn	any	1–3 months
Hungarian grazing rye (*Secale cereale*) The roots of this hardy annual grass improve drainage in clay soils, protecting them from erosion. It inhibits germination when dug in, so wait a month before sowing crops.	early autumn	any	6–7 months
White mustard (*Sinapis alba*) A half-hardy brassica, mustard makes a fast-growing weed suppressant between crops on bare soil and improves soil when dug in. Do not use where other brassicas are planned.	early spring to early autumn	fertile, well-drained	1–2 months
Crimson clover (*Trifolium incarnatum*) Fast-growing and hardy, this annual legume delivers a range of nutrients, especially nitrogen, when dug into the soil, while the pretty flowers also attract pollinators.	early spring to late summer	well-drained	2–3 months
Red clover (*Trifolium pratense*) This hardy perennial legume can be grown for a year or more to help prevent soil erosion. Cut the leaves regularly when it reaches 30cm (12in) and use as a nitrogen-rich mulch.	early spring to early autumn	any	3–18 months
Fenugreek (*Trigonella foenum-graecum*) Providing a quick boost of nutrients, this fast-growing half-hardy annual will also help to suppress weeds when grown on bare soil in between crop sowings.	early spring to late summer	well-drained	2–3 months
Field and broad beans (*Vicia faba*) Sow these hardy annual legumes in rows and release their nitrogen by digging them into the soil before the beans develop. They will also protect the soil over winter.	early to late autumn	clay	4–6 months
Vetch or winter tares (*Vicia sativa*) A hardy annual legume, vetch sown from March to August can be dug in after 2–3 months to return nitrogen to the soil; a later sowing also protects the soil from erosion over winter.	early spring to early autumn	water-retentive	2–3 months

Buckwheat

Phacelia

White mustard

Red clover

Fenugreek

WONDERFUL WORMERIES

Worms are remarkable creatures that play a crucial role in the production of healthy soils. They can eat over half their body weight in organic matter each day, and their droppings, known as casts, are rich in nutrients and microbes that help to defend plants against pests and disease. To make this compost, you will need special types of earthworm, a home for them to live in, and food to keep them active.

Wormeries transform kitchen scraps into compost with a high nutrient content.

HOW WORMERIES WORK

Using worms to make compost, known as "vermicomposting", offers a great way to recycle excess kitchen scraps that would make an ordinary compost bin too wet. Wormeries can be set up on a small balcony or patio, or even in the home, making this method perfect for those with limited outdoor space.

The worms used are not the large, pale pink burrowing earthworms that you find in garden soil, but two species, *Eisenia foetida* and *Lumbricus rubellus*, which are known variously as red or tiger worms, or brandlings. In a natural environment, they live near the surface where there are high concentrations of organic matter, such as in leafmould or under compost piles. Specialist suppliers usually offer these worms as part of a starter package, or you can buy them from fishing-tackle suppliers. You will only need to buy worms once, since they breed rapidly, given the right conditions, so you should never run out, even after you have harvested the compost.

Wormeries are usually made up of stackable trays, with a sump and tap at the base. The sump collects the worm "tea" which is produced as the worms release the moisture in the food waste you feed to them, while the tap allows you to siphon it off easily and prevents the wormery from becoming waterlogged and airless, which would kill all the inhabitants. Most suppliers also provide bedding material for the worms made from coir, which creates the right environment for them, or you can make your own from shredded paper and card. Once they are settled in, you simply keep your worms well fed with kitchen scraps, applying these in thin layers every few days, and wait for them to work their magic (for more details on how to set up a wormery, see pp.76–77).

The red worms you will need for composting are available from wormery specialists and fishing-tackle suppliers.

Fruit and vegetable peelings provide a healthy diet for composting worms.

THE PERFECT DIET

Composting worms enjoy a feast of fresh kitchen scraps such as fruit and vegetable peelings, but they are not really designed to handle woody waste, which is best composted in a conventional bin or separately (see pp.68–69). However, you can include a few soft green leaves, plant stems, and flowers. Your worms will also eat small amounts of meat, fish, and dairy products, but if you add too many the smell may attract flies. Some experts advise against adding citrus fruit peelings and onions, which can be too acidic for the worms when supplied in large volumes, but neither will harm your composters if they are included in small quantities or have been cooked. Alternatively, use a pH kit to test the compost (see p.13) and balance any acidity with alkaline materials, such as crushed eggshells, calcified seaweed, or calcium carbonate.

FOOD TO INCLUDE Fruit and vegetable peelings, raw or cooked • Loose leaf tea and coffee grounds • Paper and cardboard (shredded) • Flowers • Pet and human hair • Grass cuttings (small amounts) • Soft green garden waste (small amounts)• Crushed eggshells

FOOD TO AVOID Large amounts of meat, fish, and dairy products • Large amounts of citrus or onions (unless cooked first) • Dog and cat faeces • Glossy or plastic-coated paper products

> **TOP TIP** REMOVE SEEDS FROM FRUIT AND VEGETABLE SCRAPS BEFORE FEEDING THEM TO YOUR WORMS. MOST WILL STILL BE VIABLE AFTER COMPOSTING AND MAY GERMINATE WHEN YOU SPREAD THE FINISHED MATERIAL OVER THE SOIL.

THE NUTRIENT BENEFITS

Worm casts are rich in the main plant nutrients, containing up to five times more nitrogen, seven times more phosphorus, and over ten times more potassium than ordinary soil. Packed with beneficial microbes that protect plants from pests and diseases, they also help to condition and neutralize the soil. Use worm compost to make potting mixes (see pp.96–97), as a 2.5–5cm (1–2in) mulch on beds of flowers and crops, or apply it in a thin 1cm (½in) layer around the stems of houseplants.

The worm "tea" that you drain from the bottom of a wormery can be used as plant fertilizer. It will be richest in nutrients when at least one tray in a wormery is full of casts and it should then be diluted with ten parts water to one part worm tea before using. Any liquid produced earlier in the process will have a low nutrient content.

Use a thin layer of worm compost on the soil around your houseplants.

SETTING UP A WORMERY

Wormeries are available in a range of styles, including stainless steel models that would not look out of place in a modern kitchen or utility room. These smart units do not come cheap, but they are durable and should last for many years. If you plan to site your wormery in the garden, look out for kits with a planter at the top. While plants in the pot will not immediately benefit from the composting going on below, you can use it for flowers to attract pollinators, herbs, or vegetable plants such as a courgette or bush tomato. You can also feed the plants with worm tea or the compost when it is ready.

GETTING STARTED

Red worms prefer warm temperatures, so locate your wormery in a sheltered spot outside, close to the kitchen door to make filling it easier, or in a shed or garage. Alternatively, install one in a kitchen or utility room, but check that the model you buy is suitable for indoor composting. Collect your scraps in a separate small caddy in the kitchen and feed the worms about twice a week, adding the food in layers of no more than 5cm (2in) – too much food may result in the scraps decomposing into a wet soup, which will kill them. As a rough guide, 500g (18oz) of worms will consume about 250g (9oz) of kitchen waste each day, but remember that after a few weeks they will start to breed and you will have more to feed.

Return any worms in your harvested compost to their home in the wormery to continue their work.

Collect kitchen scraps in a caddy fitted with a lid that will reduce odours.

NEED TO KNOW

- If the top of the wormery feels wet rather than damp, drain excess liquid from the tap at the bottom and add more shredded paper and card to the feeding tray.
- If the wormery is too dry in summer, lightly water the contents.
- When using a plant pot on top, remove it to water the plant and do not use chemical fertilizers which may harm the worms if they seep down into the wormery.
- In winter, worm activity slows down and you may need to feed them less often. Move your bin to a garage or shed or wrap it in bubble plastic for insulation if it is to remain outside.

HARVESTING THE COMPOST

When the third or fourth tray in your wormery is full of worms and composting scraps, the lowest tray should be ready for harvesting. This may take up to six months or longer. The compost should be dark brown, with a woodland scent. Lift off the upper trays to remove the lowest one containing the finished compost. Set the second tray over the sump and use the emptied lower tray on top of the others when it is needed again.

In addition, drain the compost tea from the tap at the bottom every week to prevent the wormery from becoming waterlogged and airless.

HOW TO SET UP A WORMERY

YOU WILL NEED Stackable wormery •
Bedding • Shredded paper or card •
Compost and plants (optional)

1 Stand the base unit (sump) with the
tap on level ground. You may need to
raise it up on bricks or legs to make
space under the tap for a container
that will hold the liquid when it is
drained off. This unit has corrugated
rings that fit into each tray and
prevent the worms from escaping,
but not all models have these.

2 Stack the second tray on top of the
base unit and add the bedding mix
to it – you may have to soak a coir
block first and leave it to expand.
Add the worms and a couple of
handfuls of slightly rotting food
scraps from the bottom of your
kitchen caddy in one corner. Cover
and leave the worms to settle in.

3 After a week, add a 5cm (2in) layer
of fresh kitchen scraps. Chop up any
large stems such as those of broccoli
or corn cobs before including them.

4 Cover the scraps with a layer of
shredded paper and then add the lid
or planted-up pot (see step 6). A few
days later, lift up the shredded paper
to check that the worms are coping
with the waste you are giving them.
Once the worms start to breed, you
may be able to add scraps more
frequently. Continue to add layers of
kitchen scraps and shredded paper
until the first tray is full.

5 Add another corrugated ring and
composter unit on top of the first,
plus a layer of food waste. The
worms will migrate up to the new
tray to feed. Continue to add trays
when the one below is full.

6 If your wormery has a plant pot as
a lid, fill it with potting compost and
add flowers, herbs, or vegetables
such as the courgette used here.

BOKASHI COMPOSTING

For people with little or no outdoor space, bokashi composting is often advertised as a way to compost kitchen waste safely in your home. A bokashi bin is needed for this method and it can be stored in a kitchen, utility room, or garage. You can also throw in all of your food scraps, including meat, fish, and dairy, which are digested by anaerobic microbes that thrive without oxygen. However, the final product does not resemble the crumbly, soil-like compost you may be expecting, but a fermented mix of materials that have changed little in appearance from the original food you put in.

The bokashi method can be carried out in a kitchen or utility room without any unpleasant odours.

WHAT IS BOKASHI?

The term "bokashi composting" is a misnomer because it is in fact a fermentation process more akin to pickling than decomposition, which occurs in a compost bin outdoors. Bokashi is a material inoculated with harmless anaerobic bacteria called *Lactobacillus* which convert some of the carbohydrates in the food to lactic acid. The inoculant is often referred to as "Effective Microbes", or EM, and it is usually sold in the form of bran and molasses, and may also contain yeasts, fungi, and other organisms that function without air. However, unlike anaerobic composting that may occur outside, bokashi fermentation does not produce harmful gases, such as methane.

Bokashi bran is inoculated with anaerobic bacteria that pickle your food waste

THE BENEFITS OF FERMENTATION

The main benefit of the bokashi process is that you can do it indoors, close to the source of your food waste. You can also add fish, dairy, and meat products, except for large bones, and both cooked and raw foods.

Fermentation does not accelerate in warm temperatures and works equally well in summer and winter – in fact, no heat is produced as the anaerobic bacteria process the food. The bin's airtight lid eliminates odours, too. The fermentation process takes just a couple of weeks, but while this is considerably faster than even traditional hot composting methods, it is not the end of the process. After fermentation, the pickled food is composted in the garden where aerobic decomposers that live outside will get to work on it, rotting it down and releasing its nutrients in the usual manner.

A by-product of bokashi fermenting is liquid which collects at the bottom of the bin and must be drawn off every few days (see *p.81*) to prevent waterlogging. As it is very acidic, this can be used to clean drains and septic tanks. It can be also be diluted with one part

You can add dairy products such as cheese to your bokashi bin.

bokashi liquid to 100 parts water and applied to your garden or houseplants; bokashi enthusiasts use it as a very mild plant fertilizer, though some experts question its nutrient value.

USING BOKASHI FERMENTS

There are some drawbacks to this form of ecological waste processing, and disposing of the end product if you have only a small compost bin is one of them. Like any pickle, bokashi is very acidic, so you cannot use the fermented material as you would finished compost. Instead, you have to either add it in small quantities to a traditional outdoor compost bin (if you add large amounts of bokashi, the bin may become too acidic for worms and some of the other decomposers) or bury it in the garden, but not too close to plant roots, which it may burn. You must also refrain from planting over the buried material for at least two weeks, although you can sow seeds in the soil above straight away. Finding enough fallow ground in a small plot to bury your bokashi ferments could prove challenging, but once composted or buried, the pickled food will not attract vermin and should decompose within about a month – a much shorter time than raw food would break down during conventional cool composting.

Bokashi bins are quickly filled, especially if you have a family and produce a lot of kitchen waste. This may mean that you need two bins – filling one while the other ferments – or deal with any excess food waste that you cannot compost outside in another way.

> **TOP TIP** TO PREVENT A BUILD-UP OF FLUID IN YOUR BIN, WHICH CAN CAUSE PUTRID SMELLS AND BLACK OR BLUE MOULD ON THE WASTE, DRAIN IT TWICE A WEEK AND REMOVE THE CONTENTS AFTER THREE WEEKS, EVEN IF THE BIN IS NOT FULL.

Buried bokashi will decompose more quickly than untreated food waste.

THE SOIL FACTORY

Designed to appeal to people without access to outdoor space, the "soil factory" is a term coined to describe the making of soil using bokashi ferments. It does not, of course, really make new soil, which in nature takes hundreds, if not thousands, of years. The idea is to sandwich your bokashi ferment between layers of topsoil, or coir, which you can buy from a garden centre. Add 20 litres (18 quarts) of topsoil to the bottom of a bucket, then drain all the fluid from your bokashi bin and tip the ferment on top, breaking apart the waste food with a fork. Add another 20 litres (18 quarts) of soil on top and mix it with the fermented material, and finally apply a further 20 litres (18 quarts) of soil over that. The bokashi will break down and disappear within about 2–4 weeks but it will continue to decompose over time to release its nutrients. You can use this soil for houseplants and outdoor containers.

Use bokashi-enriched soil to plant up your house plants or apply it as a mulch.

USING A BOKASHI BIN

The bokashi method of fermentation is very easy to do at home and your food waste can be added to the bin in batches as it accumulates. The fermenting process may produce a white mould on the waste you throw in, which is normal, and it should smell sour, like pickled vegetables. When the fermentation process is complete, if you add the bokashi mix to your compost bin outdoors, layer it with unfermented waste such as food scraps, card, and calcium-rich plants (see p.29) to prevent the compost becoming too acidic for worms and other decomposers.

Add batches of kitchen waste with a handful of bran to the bokashi bin every few days until it is full.

INGREDIENTS FOR A BIN

Unlike outdoor composting, you should only feed your bokashi bin with food scraps – it is not designed for garden waste or cardboard. However, you can include all types of food, including meat, fish, and dairy products, but leave out large bones, which will take too long to ferment. Here are lists of what to add and what to leave out.

SUITABLE WASTE Raw and cooked fruit and vegetables, including citrus and banana peel • Raw and cooked meat and fish, including small bones • Cheese and yoghurt • Eggs • Bread • Coffee grounds, tea leaves, and torn tea bags that do not contain plastic (see p.34) • Wilted flowers • Small quantities of used paper tissues

UNSUITABLE WASTE Liquids, including vinegar, fruit juice, milk, oil, gravy, and meat juices • Teabags that contain plastic • Large bones • Animal excrement • Paper and cardboard • Metal, plastic, and glass • Medications and chemicals • Diseased plants

Raw and cooked kitchen food waste, including citrus and banana peel, and cut flowers can be added to your bin.

NEED TO KNOW
- Do not keep plastic bokashi bins outside, where they may be damaged by frost.
- Keep the bin out of direct sunlight, which could make the contents too hot for the microbes. Room temperature is best.
- You can store your bin on the counter or in a cupboard in the kitchen, in the utility room, or in a frost-free garage or shed.

HOW TO MAKE BOKASHI FERMENTS

YOU WILL NEED Bokashi bran (inoculant)
• Bokashi bin • Knife • Kitchen scraps •
Saucer or small plate • Cup to capture
the bokashi liquid

1 Scatter a handful of bokashi bran
 on the bottom of the bin over the
 drain tray. Some units come with a
 scoop to help you measure out the
 proportions of bran more accurately.

2 To speed up the process, you can cut
 up your waste into smaller pieces.
 Add a layer of scraps over the bran
 at the bottom of the bin.

3 Remove any air pockets in the mix by
 pressing down the waste firmly – you
 can use a saucer or plate to do this.

4 Scatter some more bran over the
 waste and cover the bin with the lid,
 making sure that it is sealed tightly so
 that no air can enter. Remove the lid
 only to add more waste.

5 Keep adding your waste every few
 days (store it in another small bucket
 or bag to avoid opening the bin too
 frequently, which will allow more air
 in) and remember to scatter bran
 over each layer that you include.

6 Drain the fermentation liquid from
 the bin using the tap at the bottom.
 This juice may take more than a
 week to accumulate when the bin
 is first filled but should then be
 drawn off every 3–4 days. When
 the bucket is full, scatter two large
 handfuls of bran over the final layer,
 apply the lid tightly, and leave to
 ferment for two or three weeks.
 You can then compost it in the
 garden or use it to make house
 plant soil, as described on p.79.

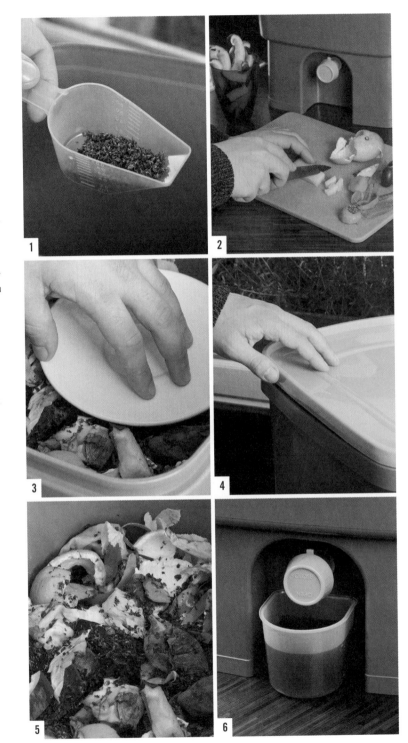

MAKING FERTILIZER TEAS

Whichever method you choose to create your compost, you can transform it into a balanced liquid fertilizer that will promote healthy plant growth. Studies show that the microbes in fertilizer made from compost, known as "tea", inhibit the growth of plant pathogens when they are sprayed on the leaves and help to bolster plants' immunity to disease when applied to the soil. If your compost is not ready to use, try comfrey or nettles from the garden instead, which both make effective tea fertilizers. These natural plant foods can replace chemical-based products that damage the environment.

Leave the compost and water to stew for a few days before straining it.

The microbes in compost teas protect plants against diseases when sprayed on the leaves.

BREWING TEA FROM HOMEMADE COMPOST

The nutrients in compost leach out when it is left to stew in water for a few days, creating a mild but effective plant fertilizer. To make the tea, you will need finished compost that looks dark brown, smells sweet like woodland soil, and has a crumbly texture (although a few half-composted twiggy bits will not cause a problem). In a cool or high-fibre heap (see pp.56–61), expect to wait a year or more for the finished product; a hot heap (see pp.54–55) will produce it much sooner.

Fill a bucket one-third full with compost and top it up with water from a water butt. If you do not have a butt, you can use chlorinated tap water if you leave it in a separate container for a day or two to allow the chlorine to dissipate first. Stir and leave the mixture to steep for three to four days, stirring occasionally. Strain the solution through muslin or an old cotton or linen shirt into a clean bucket and return any lumps to the compost bin. Dilute the remaining liquid with ten parts rainwater to one part tea, and use it to spray on your plant leaves or to drench the soil over the root zones, where it will provide nutrients to boost plants' growth. A drop of vegetable oil will help the tea to stick to the leaves when you are using it as a foliar drench.

TOP TIP USE A SPRAY BOTTLE DESIGNED TO MIST HOUSE PLANTS TO APPLY COMPOST TEA AS A FOLIAR (LEAF) FEED. STORE ANY EXCESS TEA IN A COOL, DARK PLACE AWAY FROM CHILDREN AND PETS.

MAKING COMFREY AND NETTLE TEAS

Both comfrey (*Symphytum officinale*) and nettles make excellent natural fertilizer teas: comfrey is rich in potassium (potash), while nettles are high in nitrogen. Use comfrey tea on fruit crops and potted flowers, applying it to the soil once a fortnight when fruits form or blooms are in bud. Use the nettle tea once every three weeks on leafy crops. Apply either tea as a foliar spray once or twice during the growing season on mature leaves.

To make these plant teas, use 1kg (2lb) nettles to 10 litres (2 gal) of water, or 1kg (2lb) comfrey leaves to 15 litres (3 gal) of water.

1 Collect leaves and non-flowering stems if you are also growing the plants for pollinators, or harvest after flowering.
2 Chop up the leaves and stems and pack them into a bucket or other container with a lid. Weigh them down with a brick. Add water (*see note for compost tea, opposite*) and cover. Leave comfrey to ferment for about six weeks and nettles for three or four weeks.
3 Strain the liquid into a labelled bottle with a cap – it is quite smelly – and store in a cool place away from children and pets. Dilute 1 part tea to 10 parts rainwater before applying.

Comfrey tea is rich in potash (potassium), the plant nutrient that promotes the formation of fruits such as pumpkins and squashes.

Applying a layer of compost over the soil on flowerbeds and vegetable plots and leaving the worms to take it down into the soil will improve your plants' health and productivity.

USING COMPOST

Homemade compost is most frequently used as a mulch. Spreading a layer over the soil helps to suppress weed growth, while worms and other minibeasts integrate it into the lower depths without any assistance from you. This method helps to maintain good soil structure, while enhancing its nutrient content. You can also use your compost to make seed and potting mediums. This not only saves money but lowers your carbon footprint, reducing your need for manufactured composts that contribute to plastic and air pollution during their production, packaging, and transportation.

WHEN IS COMPOST READY?

Compost can take from eight weeks to two years to mature, depending on the method, the type of bin, and the materials you include in it, but determining when your finished product is ready is partly down to personal choice. You can use a coarse-textured, semi-decomposed mix as a mulch, which worms will take into the soil to rot down further at plant root level, or wait for a finer material to develop, which may require more time in your bin but would be ideal for potting mixes and seed-sowing.

USE YOUR NOSE

Fine-textured potting compost sold in bags can give gardeners a false impression of what their homemade material should look like when it is ready to use. This can mean that you leave your compost to rot down for longer than you need to, or worry that the process is not working as it should.

The hot composting method will produce finished compost that is crumbly, spongy, and dark in colour within a few months, while the high temperatures produced also kill off pests and diseases (see pp.54–55). However, for compost to reach the same stage of decomposition in a cool heap, you may need to leave it for a year or more. If you have space for a large bin, you may wish to use the hot method rather than wait that long, but if you own a small garden and compact bin, cool composting will probably be your only option. If you can squeeze in a few bins, but do not have enough material to follow the hot composting method, you can leave one of them to decompose down to the finer-grade material suitable for potting composts (see pp.96–97), while using partly decomposed, more lumpy compost from a second bin as a mulch (see pp.90–95), and filling a third with fresh waste material.

Whichever method you employ to make your compost, the best way of testing whether it is "finished" is to use your nose – it should smell sweet and earthy, like a damp woodland. It will also be a dark brown colour and have a spongy texture, with few visible signs of the food or garden waste that you threw in at the beginning of the process. Do not be concerned if it still contains twigs and perhaps the odd corn cob or woody plant stalk – you can simply pick them out and return them to your bin for further decomposing.

Seeds will germinate and grow well in compost that is ready for use in the garden.

THE SEED TEST

One failsafe way of ensuring that your compost has decomposed to a usable level is to add a few handfuls to small pots and sow some radish seeds in them. If most of the seeds germinate and grow well, then your compost is ready to use in potting or seed composts. Radishes are generally used for this purpose because they germinate quickly, but you can sow other seeds that sprout rapidly, such as cosmos flowers. Immature compost may contain phytotoxins that kill seed embryos, resulting in failed germination.

Finished compost should be dark brown and smell like a damp woodland.

The digestive systems of worms can kill plant pathogens in a cool compost heap.

To harvest your compost from
a recycled plastic bin, lift it off to reveal
the finished material at the bottom.

TOP TIP ADD SOME FINISHED COMPOST TO THE MIX WHEN YOU REPLENISH AN EMPTIED
BIN WITH NEW MATERIAL. THE COMPOST WILL POPULATE THE CONTENTS WITH THE
BENEFICIAL MICROBES AND MINIBEASTS NEEDED TO START THE PROCESS UP AGAIN.

USING COMPOST AS PLANT FOOD

Unlike manufactured fertilizers, which will deliver exact amounts of plant nutrients, the chemical components of homemade composts depend on the materials you include in the mix. However, despite this variability, compost plays an important role in feeding plants by improving the soil structure, which in turn increases the air, water, and nutrients available to roots and promotes healthy growth.

Soil enriched with homemade compost usually contains enough nutrients to feed root crops such as carrots.

PLANT NUTRIENTS EXPLAINED

To thrive, plants require three key nutrients – nitrogen (N), phosphorus (P), and potassium (K) – as well as trace nutrients, such as iron, manganese, zinc, copper, boron, and molybdenum, which are needed in smaller quantities. You may see the letters NPK on manufactured fertilizers and composts, with numbers next to them showing the ratio of nutrients that the products contain. For example, a balanced fertilizer will have an NPK of 5:5:5, which means it has equal proportions of all three nutrients.

KEY PLANT NUTRIENTS Most plants thrive in soil that delivers these three nutrients, but some require higher doses of one particular element. For example, leafy crops need plentiful supplies of nitrogen, while flowering plants require more potassium.

Nitrogen (N) Known as the leaf-maker, this nutrient promotes healthy foliage; a deficiency causes yellowing leaves and poor growth

Potassium (K) Also known as potash, this nutrient promotes flowering and fruiting and general plant hardiness. A deficiency causes poor flowering or fruiting and the leaves may also turn yellow or purple, with brown edges

Compost usually delivers all the nutrients needed for woody plants

Phosphorus (P) This chemical promotes good root growth. Deficiencies, which will cause poor growth, are rare, except in areas with high rainfall or heavy clay

Plants require nitrogen, phosphorus, and potassium to sustain healthy growth.

FOOD FOR THOUGHT

There is no precise way of measuring the exact nutrient content of homemade compost, unless you have it tested in a laboratory. This may be a problem if you want to give your tomatoes a fix of potash (potassium) or feed the lawn with a high dose of nitrogen. Unlike many artificial fertilizers, the compost from your bin will contain relatively low levels of plant nutrients, whatever waste materials you have used to make it. However, the microbes and minibeasts it contains open up channels for air and water to pass through, which in turn makes nutrients more freely available because plant roots take up their food in a solution of water. By improving the soil in this way, compost usually delivers all the goodness garden plants need to thrive, although some crops may benefit from an additional fertilizer, such as seaweed concentrate.

Using compost as a mulch will help to provide plants with the nutrients they need for healthy growth.

SPOILED BY RICHES

The overuse of fertilizers, both in gardens and through agricultural practices, has serious consequences for the environment. Phosphates and nitrates that plants do not absorb filter down through the soil layers and pollute the groundwater, which then flows into rivers and oceans. These excessive nutrients cause algal blooms that use up the oxygen in the water, killing plants and wildlife.

Too much fertilizer can also directly harm your plants, causing "reverse osmosis", which is when the soil water contains higher concentrations of nutrients than the roots' cells, causing water and nutrients to flow out of the plant. While it is possible to overfeed with homemade composts, this is unlikely to occur if you apply a thin

mulch once a year. Mulching in spring on free-draining soils also lowers the risk of nutrients leaching out over winter.

Compost has another advantage in that it releases its nutrients over time rather than in one dose. The finished compost that you use on the garden will continue to decompose after you have applied it, and may deliver low levels of some nutrients over the course of a few years, rather than weeks. The process of decomposition also speeds up when temperatures rise during the summer, just when plants are growing quickly and need more nutrients.

Remember, too, that woodlands sustain trees and plants without additional fertilizers and many fruit and vegetable crops will thrive on lower doses than the fertilizer manufacturers recommend. Recent research also suggests that crops fed less may be more nutritious, so think twice and check if your plants are really suffering before reaching for a packet of fertilizer.

Excessive use of artificial fertilizers leads to the pollution of waterways such as rivers and streams.

WHAT IS MULCH?

The term "mulch" is used to describe a layer of organic or inorganic material which is laid over the soil to protect it. Organic mulches include homemade composts, animal manures, and wood chips, while inorganic types could be gravel, shingle, or even plastic sheets. Protecting your soil from drying out in hot, sunny weather or washing away in floods after a storm are two major benefits, but mulching with organic materials can offer even greater rewards, helping to increase the productivity of both edible and ornamental gardens as it slowly rots down further.

Spreading organic matter on the surface of the soil insulates it from fluctuating air temperatures.

Mulching helps to prevent waterlogging and soil erosion during and after heavy rain.

MULCHING BENEFITS

The practice of protecting the soil with insulating materials has been used in agriculture for a thousand years or more and takes its cue from natural processes, where leaf litter falls on to the surface (see pp.14–15). Covering the soil lowers evaporation rates and locks in moisture, while also helping to keep roots warmer and less prone to frost damage in winter. Mulches also slow down the speed at which heavy rain hits the surface, allowing the water to seep into the soil slowly, which reduces the risk of localized flooding. Whether organic or inorganic, a mulch can also help to suppress weed growth, and may even kill off invasive types such as bindweed (*Calystegia sepium*) when kept in place for a long period (see p.94).

NATURAL BLANKETS

As well as protecting the soil, organic mulches such as homemade compost and leafmould are taken down into the soil by worms, where they will continue to decompose and, as they do so, release plant nutrients (see pp.88–89). Their spongy texture also creates a cushioning effect, allowing you to tread on a compost mulch (when working on a vegetable bed, for example) without compacting the soil beneath it. Unlike inorganic mulches, you can also plant or sow seeds into a compost layer – the roots will soon reach down into the soil and stabilize the plants as the compost continues to decompose. The combined effects of worm activity, root growth, and the humus in compost, which binds soil particles together, will improve the delivery of nutrients and air to your plants, helping to increase crop yields and the vigour of ornamental plants. Long-term trials conducted in the UK showed that compost mulches applied over a seven-year period increased crop yields by 7 per cent and the size and weight of the apples grown in an orchard.

Compost mulches can help to increase crop yields by 7 per cent.

DIGGING VS NO DIGGING

Applying mulches rather than digging in compost to improve a soil is known as the "no-dig method". Traditional gardening techniques such as single- and double-digging require the gardener to dig a series of trenches deep into the soil and refill them with a mixture of the excavated soil and well-rotted compost or manure. However, recent research suggests that this practice can adversely affect the soil structure, breaking up the intricate network of fungal strands that bind the particles together and create passageways for air and water. The mycorrhizal fungi that wrap around or grow inside plant roots are also essential in feeding the majority of plants and crops, so breaking these down can affect growth too. Digging is, of course, essential in some circumstances – to add plants to the soil or for some composting methods, for example – but you should try to minimize soil disturbance as much as possible once plants are established.

Digging the soil can break up networks of fungal strands that build healthy soils by binding the particles together.

MULCHING PROBLEMS AND SOLUTIONS

Most gardeners experience few problems when they apply an organic mulch to their beds and borders. However, very occasionally a wood chip mulch may introduce a fungal disease such as honey fungus, and shredded freshly cut stems may temporarily remove nitrogen in the upper layers of the soil, as microbes that decompose the woody material use up reserves of this plant nutrient (see p.88).

The solution is to store fresh wood chips separately for 3–4 months before applying them to the soil. Signs of any fungal diseases will appear during this time, allowing you to dispose of affected materials. Leaving the chips to rot for a while also allows the decomposition that uses up nitrogen to take place away from your crops and plantings. However, if you cannot wait or have no space to store wood chips, you can still use them as a mulch around mature plants, whose roots are deeper in the soil and will not be affected by nitrogen deficiencies. Just try to make sure the trees or shrubs you have taken stems from show no signs of disease. Some studies have also found that a wood chip mulch will actually help to increase nitrogen levels in the soil over the longer term.

Plant pests such as slugs and snails may find a warm home beneath a mulch, but they will soon attract predators, such as birds and beetles, which will help to keep these molluscs in check.

TOP TIP DO NOT USE SHREDDED TIMBER OR CHIPBOARD AS A MULCH. THESE MATERIALS MAY CONTAIN ARSENIC, CHROMIUM, OR SYNTHETIC RESINS THAT WILL HARM YOUR PLANTS.

Thrushes soon seek out snails and slugs that may be hidden beneath a mulch.

USING COMPOST MULCHES

You can use all the different composts you have made at home as mulches to condition the soil, improve growth, and boost your plants' resilience to drought or freezing temperatures. Applying mulches on heavy clays prone to waterlogging will protect these soils from excessive rain and flood erosion over winter, while adding them to free-draining soils in spring will help to suppress young weed growth and lock in water, creating the perfect conditions for crops and ornamental plants to flourish.

CHOOSING MATERIALS

Homemade compost makes an excellent mulch for all types of productive and ornamental gardens, protecting and enriching the soil while also creating a stable structure. Well-rotted animal manures also make good insulating mulches (see pp.36–37), and work in a similar way to compost from a bin, though they tend to deliver slightly lower levels of some nutrients.

Leafmould is another good option, especially when used as a mulch around shrubs and trees that would naturally benefit from a layer of decomposing leaves. If you have made leafmould from conifer tree foliage, you can use it as a mulch for acid-loving plants, such as camellias and rhododendrons, grown in pots (see p.97). It will not turn an alkaline soil acidic but will help to maintain the right conditions for these potted plants.

Wood-chip mulches are a good choice for woodland gardens, too, and unlike many other organic mulches, they will not need to be topped up annually; the material will protect the soil for up to three years as it gradually rots down. Aged wood mulches (see p.91) are also water-absorbent, and release moisture into the soil, protecting newly planted trees and shrubs from drought as their roots establish. You can use fresh chips for pathways and around mature woody plants, but they may harm young specimens due to the compounds they contain, which deter animals from eating them or suppress germination so that other plants do not grow too close by.

Mulching in early spring helps to suppress weed growth.

WHEN TO APPLY

The best time to apply an organic mulch on clay soils is in the autumn when the soil is moist. Mulch after you have harvested your crops and as perennials die down in the ornamental garden – you can leave their dying foliage intact to add another protective layer on top of the mulch. Laying a mulch in autumn allows worms to bring it down into the soil before their activity slows down in winter. Worm activity also opens up channels for water to drain through, preventing run-off and flooding, which is more prevalent in clay soils.

Mulching in late winter or early spring is recommended on free-draining soils, where the nutrients in compost can be washed away by winter rains if it is applied in autumn. Spring showers will wash the nutrients down into the upper soil layers where roots are growing rapidly at this time of year.

Homemade compost is ideal for mulching young crops, while fresh wood chips can be used to deter weed growth on pathways.

APPLICATION RATES

To improve the soil structure, spread homemade compost or animal manures in a layer 2.5–5cm (1–2in) deep on ornamental beds or 7.5cm (3in) for productive plots. Apply leafmould to the same depth as compost on ornamental beds. Wood chips, which decompose more slowly, can be added to a depth of 15cm (6in) or more (see also p.95). Apply homemade compost annually to a vegetable garden and every two years to a flowerbed, or annually if the soil is dry and sandy or heavy clay. Wood chip mulches need only be replaced every three years, unless the chips are finely shredded, which may increase the rate of decomposition. Do not add mulches more frequently than recommended,

Organic mulches will boost the performance of both edible and ornamental gardens.

since too much compost or animal manure can result in a build-up of phosphorus in the soil, which will have an adverse effect on the beneficial microbes and can inhibit plants' ability to take up other nutrients. It may also cause water pollution.

HOW TO MULCH

Laying a mulch is one of the easiest ways to improve your soil, and once it is applied, you can simply let the worms do the rest of the work for you. Using a homemade mulch over the potting compost of containerized plants will benefit them, too, locking in moisture and reducing the need to water them as frequently. A healthy soil contains 3–6 per cent organic matter, so make sure that you use your homemade mulches in the right quantities, which will reduce the risk of excess nutrients leaching into and polluting the groundwater.

A compost mulch will protect plants in hanging baskets from drying out.

MULCHING A BED

You can apply a mulch to a whole bed or spot mulch around key plants that will benefit from weed suppression and moisture retention. Perennials and most crops will simply grow through a layer of compost, but take care not to smother low-growing plants and leave a space around shrubs to prevent the damp material from rotting their woody stems.

To achieve an even layer, level up undulating ground by removing the soil from raised areas and using it to fill the hollows. Before laying a mulch, dig out pernicious weeds such as brambles and docks, which will be undeterred by a few centimetres of organic material, as well as tall weeds that the material will not completely cover. Annual weed seedlings will die under a blanket of mulch.

Lay your mulch after rain has fallen, on soil that is neither waterlogged nor frozen – the material's insulating effect will retain moisture but can equally prolong icy conditions. Use a shovel to apply the mulch and rake it over the surface to the depth you require (see p.93), taking care not to compact the soil by standing on it as you do so.

TOP TIP DAMP COMPOST MULCHES WILL CAUSE THE STEMS AND LEAVES OF MEDITERRANEAN HERBS, SUCH AS THYME AND SANTOLINA, TO DECAY. USE A LAYER OF GRAVEL OR PEBBLES AROUND THESE PLANTS INSTEAD.

Cover beds of vegetables with compost mulches, but leave gaps around Mediterranean shrubs such as lavender.

CLEARING WEEDS

If you want to use a mulch to clear weeds from a new vegetable plot or flowerbed while improving the soil at the same time, you will need to use a slightly different technique. Cover the area with a layer of thick cardboard or two layers of thinner card, making sure there are no gaps and all light is excluded from the soil. Then add 10cm (4in) of well-rotted compost or wood chips on top.

After two or three months, the cardboard will start to decay and persistent weeds may begin to grow through the mulch again. Push the compost or chips to one side, cut down the weeds' top growth and replenish the card. Then replace the compost or chips over the new cardboard layer. This will weaken the weeds' growth as they will be unable to photosynthesize and produce energy from the sun. Continue with this regime every few months until you cannot see any live white roots when you peel back the card. If you start this process in early spring, you should have a weed-free bed by early autumn. Finally, leave both card and compost in place to continue to break down and plant up your clean bed in spring.

LAYING WOOD CHIPS

The slow decomposition of wood chips means that you can use thick mulches to suppress weeds without any risk of excess nutrients leaching into and polluting waterways (see p.93). Cut down the top growth of weeds on the bed and then apply mulch to a depth of 15–30cm (6–12in), which will exclude light and kill the plants beneath. Most gardens will not produce sufficient waste wood to cover a large bed, but you could ask local tree surgeons if you can collect chips from them. Use this technique around mature plants and on new beds where weeds are causing problems – you may need to cut back any new growth that struggles through the mulch, but the weeds should die within 12 months.

Plastic mulches reduce weed growth and warm the soil, but they are also sources of pollution in the garden.

Thick layers of wood chips will suppress weeds while very gradually decomposing to enrich the soil beneath.

PLASTIC WARNING

Some experts suggest laying black polythene or landscape fabric over your beds as a mulch to eliminate weeds and warm the soil in spring. While these products form a uniform blanket that excludes the light that weeds need to grow, they also introduce plastic into the garden, which is polluting during its manufacture and when it ends up in landfill. If you decide to use a plastic mulch to suppress weeds, buy a high-grade material that can be reused year after year.

MULCHING POTTED PLANTS

Gardeners frequently neglect to add a mulch to their container plantings, though it will provide the same benefits that make it valuable on open ground. In fact, mulching plants in pots with homemade compost or leafmould can significantly reduce their watering requirements, which will both save you time and help to minimize the use of this increasingly precious resource. Add a mulch layer 2.5–5cm (1–2in) deep over the potting compost after planting and watering, keeping the material clear of woody tree or shrub stems to avoid rotting. Mulching up to the stems of most perennials and annuals will do them no harm.

Hydrangeas in pots benefit from mulches, which help to conserve moisture.

NEED TO KNOW

- You can sow large vegetable and flower seeds into a well-rotted compost mulch as soon as it has been laid in spring or autumn.
- Tiny seeds may not germinate in a lumpy mulch, so apply a layer of homemade seed compost on top and sow into that.
- Do not sow seeds in wood chip mulches, especially if they have been freshly cut, as they may inhibit germination rates. You can, however, plant into the soil beneath an aged wood mulch, as long as it is not too deep and won't swamp the young plants.

MAKING SEED AND POTTING COMPOSTS

Combining homemade composts and leafmould with garden soil is a quick and easy way to make your own potting mixes. On its own, garden soil may not contain sufficient nutrients to support plants grown in containers, but the plant food in your own products helps to make up for these deficiencies. Seed and cutting composts can also be made using your homemade composts, together with sand or grit.

Herbs require free-draining compost that contains horticultural sand or grit, as well as compost and leafmould.

HOMEMADE MIXES

There are many benefits to making your own potting composts, aside from the satisfaction of creating them with homemade materials harvested from your bin or wormery. You can minimize waste by only making enough to suit your needs – as with all composts, homemade potting mixes should not be stored for more than a few months, since their quality can decline over time. Using your own materials also avoids buying plastic-wrapped products, some of which contain peat. As the extraction of peat threatens rare and fragile peat-bog ecosystems, it is important to cut down on its use.

NEED TO KNOW
- While homemade composts are generally safe to handle, make sure any cuts or wounds are completely covered.
- Wash your hands thoroughly after making potting composts.

Leafmould (left), compost from your bin (centre), and horticultural sand (right), together with soil from the garden, are all you need for a variety of potting mixes.

SEED AND POTTING-ON COMPOSTS

Germination rates are usually better in growing mediums that are free-draining and contain low levels of nutrients. For seed mixes, you can include garden soil but it will need to be pasteurized first in order to kill any pests and diseases that may threaten your seedlings. To do this, spread a 10cm (4in) layer on a baking tray and bake in a preheated oven at 80°C (176°F) for 30 minutes – it may smell quite potent. Remove it from the oven and leave to cool.

For a simple seed compost, use well-matured, two-year-old sieved leafmould on its own, or mix one part pasteurized soil, one part leafmould, and one part horticultural sand. As the seedlings develop and require potting on into larger containers, they will also require more nutrients. For plants at this stage of growth, mix together one part pasteurized garden soil, one part leafmould, and one part sieved compost from a bin or wormery.

Sieve homemade compost and combine it with pasteurized soil plus leafmould to make a seedling mix.

COMPOST RECIPES

Most plants grown as annuals, such as summer bedding and spring bulbs, will be happy in an equal mix of homemade compost, unpasteurized garden soil, and leafmould. For more permanent plantings, such as perennials and shrubs, you can omit the leafmould and use a 50:50 mix of compost and soil.

For plants that prefer free-draining conditions, such as Mediterranean herbs, alpines, and succulents, make up a grittier mix by combining one part unpasteurized soil, one part homemade compost or leafmould, and one part horticultural grit or sand, or vermiculite.

Work horticultural sand or grit into a soil and leafmould mix to plant up pots of Mediterranean herbs.

MIXES FOR ACID-LOVERS

Plants such as rhododendrons, camellias, and pieris need an acidic (ericaceous) soil (see p.13) in order to thrive and will not be too happy in the homemade potting mixes used for other plants. To create the particular conditions that they require, combine one part of a two-year-old acidic leafmould, made from pine and other conifer tree needles (see p.67), with one part soil and one part homemade compost. If you do not have conifers growing close at hand, ask friends or neighbours if they have any needles that you can use.

You may find that the leaves of your plants turn yellow (a condition called chlorosis) if the soil in a pot becomes too alkaline over time. To help prevent this, apply a 2.5cm (1in) mulch of the acidic leafmould each year in spring on top of the compost, leaving a gap around the plants' stems.

Collect pine needles to make an acidic leafmould to add to pots of rhododendrons and camellias.

MAINTAINING A LUSH LAWN

Green lawns can be difficult to maintain in summer without watering and the use of artificial fertilizers, but composting the clippings can provide a more eco-friendly maintenance solution. Grass releases plant nutrients and moisture as it decomposes, which means that when the clippings are left to rot down on the soil between the leaves, they soon help to produce a healthy, lush lawn.

Grass clippings can boost the drought-tolerance of a lawn.

SELF-COMPOSTING CLIPPINGS

The easiest way to ensure that a lawn has the nutrients and moisture needed for healthy growth is to mow it and leave the clippings where they lie. Grass clippings will replenish your lawn with at least 25 per cent of the nutrients it requires, thereby reducing the need for artificial fertilizers. This helps to lower your carbon footprint and reduce the use of fertilizers, which can damage the environment by leaching into ground water and then polluting rivers and oceans.

The aim of this composting method is to leave the mowings to settle on the soil between the grass blades, where they will form a protective layer, helping to reduce weed growth and conserve moisture by reducing evaporation rates. As they decompose, they will also be taken down into the soil by worms, where they will release their nutrients and feed the grass roots.

To prevent your lawn being engulfed by a soggy mass of clippings, which will damage the grass, make sure that your mower blades are sharp and on their highest setting. Remove just one-third of the length of the grass, or about 2.5cm (1in), each time you mow. This may mean cutting the lawn more than once a week in spring and summer, but since you do not have to pick up the clippings, it should be quite an easy task. To support the taller grass leaves, the plants develop longer roots that reach down into the lower depths of soil where moisture collects, thereby providing even more protection against periods of drought.

If you find your lawn looking a little lacklustre, check that the depth of decomposing grass clippings, known as thatch, has not exceeded about 1cm (½in). This may be inhibiting the free flow of air into the soil and preventing the new clippings on top from coming into contact with the decomposing microbes in the soil. To rectify this problem, rake up some of the thatch and add it in thin layers to a compost bin or use as a mulch on your beds (see p.119), as long as you have not recently treated the lawn with herbicides such as a weed and feed product.

Mow the grass with the blades on the highest setting and leave the clippings to settle on the soil between the leaves.

TOP TIP DO NOT MOW LAWNS AFTER RAIN BECAUSE THE WET CUTTINGS MAY NOT BE EASY TO DISTRIBUTE EVENLY. THEY CAN FORM A DENSE MAT THAT SMOTHERS THE GRASS AND PREVENTS THE SOIL FROM ABSORBING AIR AND WATER.

FEEDING THE LAWN WITH COMPOST

If you prefer a more manicured lawn with shorter grass than is required for self-composting the clippings (see *opposite*), you can maintain it using homemade compost instead. Not only will the compost help to improve the soil structure, which in turn will alleviate waterlogging and reduce moss growth, it will also deliver essential nutrients to encourage healthy growth. Top dressings of compost are traditionally applied in the autumn, when they encourage good root growth and improve drainage.

However, new studies show that lighter, more frequent applications may work too, starting in spring as the grass begins to grow again. To apply homemade compost, cut the lawn to about 2.5cm (1in) in height to expose the soil between the grass blades, then rake it to remove dead leaves and debris. Sieve well-rotted compost into a bucket, scatter it over the lawn to create a thin layer of about 1cm (½in), and use a broom to distribute it evenly. Repeat this process every month or two until early autumn when grass growth begins to slow.

Use a broom to work the compost into the soil between the blades of grass.

LEAVING LAWNS TO FLOWER

To increase biodiversity and encourage pollinators into your garden, transform your lawn into a wildflower meadow. Simply leave the grasses and flowers in the lawn to grow taller and bloom; you can also add wildflower plug plants or sow seeds on the surface of the soil in spring. Mow your meadow annually in late summer after the grasses and flowers have set seed, leaving the clippings *in situ* for a few days to allow the seeds to settle on the ground. Your lawn mower may not be able to cope with long grass, in which case use a rotary mower or an old-fashioned scythe. If the grasses are dominating the flowers, try mowing the meadow twice more throughout the autumn and remove the clippings. After the main summer cut, collect the hay to use as a mulch or add it to your compost heap. These older stems have a high carbon content and are counted as browns, unlike the lush green nitrogen-rich growth of a lawn. They can therefore be added to a heap to balance grass clippings and prevent the compost from becoming too wet.

Making a meadow eliminates the problems associated with composting fresh green grass clippings.

ON THE MOVE

One way to save time and effort when composting is to place your compost bin on the bed or border that is most in need of the finished material, thereby eliminating the need to transfer the compost from a heap located elsewhere to its final position. A fallow area in a flower garden or on a vegetable plot would be the perfect place to install your bin, so that any nutrients from the decomposing material seep into the soil exactly where they are required. This method is particularly useful for gardeners with limited mobility, but anyone can benefit if they have space.

Locate your bin on a vegetable bed with soil that needs revitalizing with some homemade compost.

Disguise your bin on a bed or border in an ornamental garden by hiding it behind tall flowering plants.

SIMPLE SOLUTION

Composting *in situ* is a great choice if you have spare capacity in a bed or border that you do not mind giving up for a year while the compost matures. Setting up a bin on a productive bed in the vegetable garden, where crops are more important than aesthetics, will deliver many benefits. For example, if you are practising crop rotation, composting *in situ* would help to improve the soil in an area where you have just harvested hungry crops such as brassicas. The finished compost will then revitalize the soil for a follow-on crop of root vegetables such as carrots and potatoes.

It may also be a good solution in a large decorative space, where you could compost *in situ* in a quiet area out of sight from the house where you plan to plant trees or shrubs. However, this method may not be the best option in a small flower garden where a bin could detract from the plants or there is no room for one on narrow beds or borders. Nevertheless, if the idea appeals, you could try designing a small space for composting where the bin is disguised behind tall flowering plants. Just make sure that it will not be in deep shade, which will slow down the composting process (see *opposite*).

A bin with a hatch allows you to monitor when the compost is ready.

CHOOSING AND MOVING BINS

Lightweight, portable bins such as those made from recycled plastic are ideal for *in situ* composting. A stackable wooden model could work, too, if it is easy to dismantle and move to a new position, but a large bin for hot composting would probably be too difficult to relocate. Once your bin is in place, simply make your compost in the usual way and leave it to decompose for up to a year, if you are using the cool or high-fibre method (*see pp.56–61*). When your compost is ready, lift off the bin,

spread the finished material over the bed to form a mulch, and move the bin to the next area that needs improving. Any uncomposted material can be added to the bin once it's in its new position. Then fill the bin again and repeat the process.

You may be able to empty the bin more frequently if you only have a small space to improve. Where this is the case, lift the bin when half of the contents have broken down, which will take less time. Remember, too, that a compost mulch will continue to decompose on the soil surface, so do not worry if your product still contains a few lumps and twigs.

Composting will be quicker in a sunny spot, but you may prefer to use that area for growing crops and flowers.

TOP TIP TIGER OR BRANDLING WORMS, WHICH ARE SOLD FOR USE IN WORMERIES, CAN BE ADDED TO A REGULAR COMPOST BIN TOO, WHERE THEY WILL HELP TO SPEED UP THE COMPOSTING PROCESS.

PLANTING UP YOUR COMPOST HEAP

Once your heap has started to cool down and mature, you can plant crops or flowers directly on it to take advantage of the warmth and fertility of the compost. This is a great way to boost the productivity of your plot and provide a banquet for beneficial insects while your compost matures. Some plants, such as tomatoes, may appear without any help from you, their seeds deposited in bird droppings.

Nasturtiums will form a carpet of edible leaves and flowers on the top of a bin.

Winter and summer squashes enjoy the rich fertility of a compost heap.

HOW TO PLANT

After your bin or heap is full, wait at least two months before planting. It is best to plant seedlings rather than sow seeds directly in the heap, because the fertile compost will reduce germination rates. Sow seeds of your chosen crops and flowers indoors in spring, and plant them out once they are well established; you may have to pot them on a couple of times after sowing. Water your plants, just as if you were growing them in soil. Once your crops are harvested or the flowers finished, turn the plants back into the pile to be composted.

WHAT TO PLANT

Numerous plants and crops will thrive on a compost heap. Nasturtiums often spring up of their own accord from seeds in old potting mixes added to the heap, or through bird droppings. If so, consider yourself fortunate: their flowers will attract pollinators into your garden, and both their blooms and leaves are edible, adding a spicy kick to salads. If you want to continue the floral theme, try plunging biodegradable pots of petunias and sunflowers into the mix to create a flowery heap – the pots soon break down, allowing the roots to escape and soak up the nutrients.

If you are more interested in edible crops, try planting melons, courgettes, pumpkins, aubergines, and trailing tomatoes, such as small cherry types. These fruiting vegetables love the warmth and fertility of a compost heap, and once established will soon form large, productive plants. They all require sun, however, so this idea is only recommended if your heap is situated in a warm, sunny, and sheltered spot.

A layer of straw will help to keep courgette fruits dry as they develop.

The compost heap is an ideal place to accommodate large plants,
such as courgettes, that you might otherwise struggle to fit into your plot.

Making seed compost from your homemade material and sowing in biodegradable pots allows you to raise your plants without using any plastic or other products that would go to landfill.

COMPOST PLANTING PROJECTS

Choose from the easy sowing and planting projects in this chapter to raise delicious fruit and vegetable crops and enhance your ornamental garden. Homemade compost will not only deliver excellent results by helping to condition the soil and create a healthy environment for your plants, it will also reduce or eliminate the need for chemical fertilizers, the residues of which can enter the water table and pollute rivers and oceans. You can use your black gold to boost the performance of all types of plants, from spring bulbs to trees and shrubs, and even tender house plants.

SOWING SEEDS

Raising flowering plants and crops from seed in homemade potting mixes is a cost-effective way of filling your garden with flowers and feeding your household. You can buy seeds from a reputable supplier or collect them from your existing plants, which will save you even more money and reduce your carbon footprint further, too. The most reliable method is to sow seeds in pots under cover in spring or autumn, which protects them from pest damage and the weather – you will not need any special equipment to bring them to life.

Eco-friendly containers such as wooden trays and terracotta pots are ideal for raising plants sown from seed.

The shape and colour of plants raised from bought seeds is more predictable than those taken from your own plants.

BUYING SEED

Before buying new seeds, first calculate the number of plants you require. Seed deteriorates over time and is best sown fresh, so if you bulk-buy you may have to throw some away if you cannot use all your purchases in the first year.

If you want specific plant cultivars, it is best to buy new seeds rather than collect them from your existing plants. This is because they may be F1 hybrids, which will have been bred to produce a specific flower or fruit colour, for example. If you take seed from one of these hybrids, the offspring may not look or perform like its parent.

COLLECTING SEED

Taking seed from unhybridized plant varieties could not be easier. Wait until your flowers have formed pods or seedheads, which protect the seeds while they ripen and usually turn from green to black, brown, or red when their cargo is about to be released. Then take a paper bag and tap the seedhead gently above it so that the seeds fall into it, or cut off the whole pod and place it in the bag. Tip the seeds on to a clean, dry surface and remove any bits of seed pod or other debris (chaff), which may harbour pests or diseases.

To collect the seeds from soft fruits and fruiting vegetables, such as tomatoes, remove the fruit from the plant, scrape or scoop out the seeds, and place them in a kitchen sieve. Wash off the flesh, then leave the cleaned seeds to dry in a warm place. Pea and bean pods can be left on the plant to ripen, or removed when dry and placed in a warm area to continue ripening.

Collect your seed when the pods have turned brown, black, or red and rattle when shaken.

HOW TO SOW SEED

Sow seed in pots or trays indoors in spring or, if hardy, you can sow them in autumn and keep them in a cold frame or a sheltered spot over winter.

YOU WILL NEED Biodegradable or recycled pots or seed trays • Homemade seed compost • Bought or harvested seed • Labels • Tray with transparent lid or propagator (for plants that need heat)

1 Fill the pots or trays with homemade seed compost (see p.97) Press down lightly to remove any large air gaps. Sow the seed sparingly at the depth given on the packet. If you have harvested seed and do not have this information, plant the seeds at a depth two or three times their diameter. Tiny seeds are best sown on the surface and covered with a thin layer of compost.

2 Label the pots and keep them in a warm, light place or, if hardy, store them in a cold frame or sheltered area outside. Place those that need heat to germinate in a propagator, or in a tray with a clear lid on a warm windowsill. Water regularly.

3 Repot congested seedlings after they have produced a few sets of leaves. This is known as "pricking out". Gently hold the seedling by a leaf and use a small spoon to coax the roots out of the compost, then place it in a pot of fresh compost to grow on.

4 Accustom the young seedlings to outdoor temperatures by placing the pots or trays outside during the day and bringing them in again at night for a couple of weeks before planting out. Known as "hardening off", this should be done no earlier than two weeks before the last frosts in late spring for half-hardy or tender plants. Plant outside in the ground or in their final pots when the seedlings are growing well and have developed sturdy stems.

HARDY, HALF-HARDY, AND TENDER SEEDS

Plants that are described as hardy will survive temperatures below freezing point; others are known as half-hardy and will die when temperatures fall below 0°C (32°F). Tender plants will not survive in temperatures below 10–13°C (50–55°F). Collected hardy plant seed, or packets that have been opened, can be stored in an airtight container in a refrigerator until ready to use. Store half-hardy and tender seeds in a cool, dry place that is just above the lowest recommended temperature for those plants.

Half-hardy seeds such as basil and lettuce must be kept safe from frosts.

MAKING A MIXED FLOWERBED

One of the great joys of gardening is growing seasonal flowers right outside your back door. With the help of your homemade compost you can make a new bed in a weekend, and when planned carefully, the flowers and shrubs you plant will offer an evolving picture throughout the year. Wildlife will benefit, too, as the blooms draw in bees while seeds and berried plants offer food and shelter for birds.

Foxgloves thrive in the part shade at the edge of a tree canopy. The blue alkanet in front prefers a spot in full sun.

SITING YOUR BED

You can make a flowerbed or border almost anywhere in the garden if you choose the right plants for your site (see *opposite*). Many popular annual and perennial plants, such as cosmos, snapdragons (*Antirrhinum*), delphiniums, lupins, and salvias prefer a sunny site, but if you are planning a bed in shade, there are other beauties to choose from, including cranesbill (*Geranium*), foxgloves (*Digitalis*) and ferns. The size of your bed is another important consideration. Small or skinny beds cannot accommodate enough plants for a continuous seasonal display, so make yours as large as possible – at least 1m (3ft) square is a good benchmark, but the bigger the better.

Roses, salvias, and verbascums will all thrive in a sheltered, sunny bed.

Before you begin planting, mulch your bed with a layer of homemade compost to improve all soil types.

PREPARING A BED

The best time to make a new bed is in early spring or autumn. First, mark out the bed or border using a length of hosepipe to create a curved shape, or pegs and string if you want a more formal square or rectangle. String attached to a central peg can help you to define a perfect circular bed. If you are converting a lawn into a bed, either dig up the turf and compost it (see *p.71*), or try the lasagne compost method either in autumn (see *pp.64–65*), which will kill off the grass and deliver an enriched soil to plant up the following year, or in early spring for an autumn planting. Before planting any bed, dig out perennial weeds and remove stones and debris.

To improve all soil types, particularly heavy waterlogged clay and fast-draining sandy soil, add a 5cm (2in) mulch of homemade compost. This will not deliver immediate results, so select plants adapted to your soil conditions at first. Applying a mulch annually will gradually improve the ground and your plant range will widen after a few years. Choose plants suited to your particular site from the lists opposite or ask a reputable nursery for advice.

PLANTING OUT

Set out your plants on the bed in their pots first, making sure that they all have adequate space to grow. Most perennials and almost all woody plants should be planted at the same depth as they were growing in their original pots. A few drought-lovers such as lavender and verbascums can be planted a little proud of the surface, with a mound around their roots so water drains away from them. Water your plants before transferring them to the bed and firm around the stems gently afterwards to remove large air gaps. Finally, water them well.

Use a cane to check that your plants will be at the same depth in the soil as they were in their original pots.

SELECTING PLANTS

When choosing your plants, always check that they will thrive in your garden conditions and take note of their final heights and spreads. One common mistake is to set young plants at the front of a bed in spring only to find they have grown into giants by the end of the summer. Assessing final sizes is particularly important when selecting shrubs, which will be more difficult than perennials to move once they have become established.

Also check how much sunlight falls on your bed. Take photographs of it at different times of the day and during different seasons to help you make the best plant choices: shade-lovers that are planted in sun may scorch in the heat, while those that prefer sun but are planted in shade will stretch to find the light and may not flower. Many plants are tolerant of part shade, which means they must also receive a few hours of sunlight each day – check the plant labels for exact guidance for individual plants. The list below is a selection of easy-care plants for different aspects.

A = *annual*; B = *bulb*; Bi = *biennial*; P = *perennial*; S = *shrub*

PLANTS FOR SUN *Alstroemeria* hybrids P • Alkanet (*Anchusa azurea*) P • Cosmos (*Cosmos bipinnatus*) A • Globe thistle (*Echinops ritro*) P • Mexican fleabane (*Erigeron karvinskianus*) P • Sea holly (*Eryngium* species) P • Avens (*Geum*) P • *Hebe* species S • Perennial sunflower (*Helianthus* species) P • Stonecrop (*Hylotelephium spectabile*) P • Lavender (*Lavandula* species) S • Shasta daisy (*Leucanthemum* × *superbum*) P • Catmint (*Nepeta* species) P • *Penstemon* species P • *Perovskia* species S • Rose (*Rosa* species and cultivars) S • Sage (*Salvia* × *sylvestris*) P • Lamb's ears (*Stachys byzantina*) P • Tulip (*Tulipa* species and cultivars) B • *Verbascum* species P

PLANTS FOR PART SHADE Ornamental garlic (*Allium* species) B • Japanese anemone (*Anemone* × *hybrida*) P • Wood anemone (*Anemone nemorosa*) B • *Campanula* species P • Choisya ternata S • Montbretia (*Crocosmia* species) P • Foxglove (*Digitalis purpurea*) Bi • *Fatsia japonica* S • Hardy fuchsia (*Fuchsia magellanica*) S • Cranesbill (*Geranium* species) P • Witch hazel (*Hamamelis* × *intermedia*) S • St John's wort (*Hypericum*) S • Bleeding heart (*Lamprocapnos spectabilis*) P • Grape hyacinth (*Muscari*) B • Daffodil (*Narcissus*) B • Tobacco plant (*Nicotiana*) A • Bistort (*Persicaria bistorta*) P • Lesser periwinkle (*Vinca minor*) P

PLANTS FOR SHADE Spotted laurel (*Aucuba* species) S • Male fern (*Dryopteris filix-mas*) P • Wood spurge (*Euphorbia amygdaloides* var. *robbiae*) P • Balkan cranesbill (*Geranium macrorrhizum*) P • Hellebore (*Helleborus* species) P • *Hosta* species P • Dead nettle (*Lamium maculatum*) P • *Mahonia* × *media* S • Golden tassel fern (*Polystichum polyblepharum*) P • Sweet box (*Sarcococca confusa*) S

Alstroemeria INDIAN SUMMER

Cosmos bipinnatus 'Antiquity'

Fuchsia magellanica var. gracilis 'Aurea'

Hypericum bellum

Lamium maculatum f. album

CREATING A PLOT FOR CROPS

Many crops are hungry, thirsty plants that benefit from soil improved with a homemade compost. Either use it as mulch on a vegetable plot or, if your soil is poor or stony, make a simple raised bed and fill it with compost and topsoil to create the optimum conditions. Plant your beds with the crops you love to eat and those that are difficult to find in the shops, planning for harvests all year round.

Herbs, flowers, and tomatoes will thrive in a bed of homemade compost, which provides the nutrients and free-draining conditions they need.

LOCATING YOUR BED

Most vegetable and fruit crops thrive in sunshine, so install your bed in the brightest spot in your garden or allotment. A sheltered location is ideal, too, and will help to prevent tall crops such as sweetcorn from being blown over or tender plants failing in cold conditions. To reduce wind speeds, try installing willow hurdle fencing a few metres from your plot on the side of the prevailing wind, or plant a mixed wildlife hedge, using hornbeam, hazel, and hawthorn. If possible, locate your bed close to a water source.

Choose a sunny, sheltered site for your productive raised beds.

Fast-growing lettuces can be sown between slower-maturing crops.

CROPS FOR SMALL BEDS

Many crops are easy to grow in small spaces. One or two courgette plants will feed a family, while leeks and onions usually produce a good harvest, given a sunny spot. Radishes, salad onions, and lettuces are quick and easy, cropping just a few weeks after sowing. You can also squeeze them between larger, slow-maturing plants such as sweetcorn; known as "intercropping", this helps you make the most of a small bed. Members of the cabbage family, including Brussels sprouts, turnips, and kale as well as cabbages, are known as brassicas and are also easy to grow, if you cover them with insect-proof netting to prevent cabbage-white butterfly larvae from devouring the plants.

FRUITFUL THINKING

Raised beds make good homes for soft fruits such as strawberries, raspberries, gooseberries, and redcurrants. These crops are ideal for beginners, because they produce a harvest on the same plant for many years and generally require less work than vegetables. However, blackcurrants and blackberries may grow too big for a raised bed and are best planted in open ground, while blueberries require acid soil, so you will need to create a separate bed for them and fill it with homemade ericaceous compost (see p.97).

Redcurrants grow on compact bushes that are suitable for a sunny raised bed.

MAKING A SIMPLE RAISED BED

Only basic DIY skills are needed to make this simple timber-framed raised bed. The wood may be easily sourced from a freecycle website – just make sure it has not been treated with harmful chemicals, such as creosote.

YOU WILL NEED 4 wooden planks, such as decking boards, and some offcuts • saw • workbench (optional) • clamp • builder's square • screwdriver • stainless steel screws • spade • rake • lump hammer • 4 pointed timber stakes • small axe (optional)

1 Cut the wood to your preferred size. Screw the planks together on a level surface, such as a work bench or patio, to create simple butt joints. Use a clamp to secure the sides and a builder's square to ensure the corners are at 90 degrees.
2 Using offcuts, attach timber diagonals to support the frame while you move it into position. Level the ground in the area where you plan to locate your bed, then set the frame in place.
3 Using the lump hammer, drive a stake 30–45cm (12–18in) into the ground at each corner. This is easier if the stakes have pointed ends – you can buy these or make a point using a small axe. Tall stakes will allow you to drape netting over them to protect crops vulnerable to flying pests, or for others, cut the stakes before installing them so that they are a little lower than the frame.
4 Unscrew the cross bars carefully, then screw the timber frame to each of the stakes to give it stability.
5 Fill your bed with a mix of compost and topsoil, and rake it to create a smooth surface.
6 Plant up with your favourite crops in spring. Once you have harvested them in autumn, top up the bed with a compost mulch (see pp.94).

TOP TIP INSTEAD OF FILLING YOUR BED WITH FINISHED COMPOST FROM YOUR BIN, YOU CAN TRY THE LASAGNE COMPOSTING METHOD (*SEE PP.64–65*) IN AUTUMN. THIS WILL DECOMPOSE OVER WINTER, READY FOR PLANTING IN SPRING.

PLANTING ORNAMENTAL CONTAINERS

Pots filled with seasonal flowers bring cheer to patios, balconies, and terraces and can be tucked into a flagging border to brighten it up before or after the plants in the ground have bloomed. Container displays are easy to make using homemade composts too – just remember that plants grown in pots require more watering than those in the ground, so make sure you have time to care for them.

Succulents will thrive in small pots filled with a mixture of homemade potting compost, garden soil and grit.

Woven baskets make eco-friendly containers but may rot after a few years.

Glazed clay pots set off displays of summer bedding plants to perfection.

Modern aluminium containers are a good choice for a partly shaded site.

CHOOSING POTS

Before buying a pot, choose the plants you wish to grow and match them with a container that will accommodate the size of their root balls. Also consider how much time you will have to care for them, since most potted plants need watering 2–3 times a week during the summer. Larger pots, which hold more potting mix and therefore more moisture, generally require less attention than small containers, so if your time is limited, opt for the biggest you can fit into your space. Plant up heavy containers in situ, so that you will not have to move them when they are filled with compost and plants.

Pots made from terracotta are a good choice for many plants, but they are porous and may crack in winter if they do not come with a frost-proof guarantee. Metal containers will sail through the cold seasons without a problem and can be recycled easily, but they may get too hot and burn plant roots if placed in a sunny spot in summer. Stone troughs are tough and beautiful but heavy to lift, while plastic pots are best avoided if you want to keep your carbon footprint low; plastics produce high levels of pollution during their manufacture and are not biodegradable, although some can be recycled. Wooden boxes, half-barrels and baskets are decorative, eco-friendly options, and will last for a few years.

Summer bedding can be planted in a mix of your compost, leafmould, and soil.

PREPARING A CONTAINER

Whatever type of container you choose, make sure it has holes at the bottom to prevent waterlogging, and raise it up on "feet" that allow water to drain out easily. Also choose the right potting mixes for your plants. Bulbs and summer bedding plants will grow well in a combination of homemade compost, garden soil, and leafmould, while drought-loving plants, such as lavender, succulents, and alpines, will require a free-draining medium with additional horticultural sand or grit. Large, woody plants, such as hydrangeas, roses, and bay trees, will thrive in a 50:50 mix of compost and garden soil (see *pp.96–97*).

Thirsty plants such as hydrangeas benefit from a mulch laid over the potting compost to lock in moisture.

SUCCESSFUL PLANTING

After planting, make sure there is a gap of at least 2.5cm (1in) between the potting mix and the rim of the container. This will allow water to accumulate and seep into the growing medium, rather than spilling over the top of the pot and leaving the soil dry.

You can pack spring and summer bedding plants together more closely in a pot than you would do in the ground on account of the richer growing conditions that potting mixes provide. Shrubs, annuals, and perennial plants should be planted to the same depth they were growing at in their original pots. They will also benefit from a 2.5cm (1in) mulch of compost or leafmould on top of the potting mix to help preserve moisture, but leave a gap around the stems of woody plants to prevent the wet material from rotting them. A compost mulch will also deliver extra nutrients as it breaks down – reapply it annually each spring. Use grit to mulch alpines and succulents to keep their stems dry.

REACH FOR THE SKY

Climbing plants such as patio clematis and compact forms of honeysuckle (*Lonicera*) can be grown in large containers in a 50:50 mix of homemade compost and garden soil. Add a piece of trellis at the back of the pot, or a pyramid made from a tripod of canes in the centre of it, and attach the climbing stems to their support with soft twine. If the final height of your climbers will go beyond that of the support, set your pot next to a fence or wall. Fix sturdy wires horizontally to the vertical surface at about 30–45cm (12–18in) intervals and, if necessary, attach the stems as they grow – most climbers will cling to the wires of their own accord.

Trellis panels will provide the flexible stems of climbers with support.

Compact clematis such as OOH LA LA can be grown up a tripod in a large pot.

> **TOP TIP** DURING THE SUMMER, FEED YOUR POTTED BEDDING PLANTS EVERY 2–3 WEEKS WITH TEAS MADE EITHER FROM PLANTS OR YOUR OWN COMPOST (*SEE PP.82-83*).

PLANTING A FRUIT BASKET

Strawberries are among the easiest soft fruits to grow, and are a great choice for small spaces, where they can be planted in the ground or in pots and hanging baskets. The benefits of raising the fruits off the ground are that it protects them from pests such as mice and slugs while also making picking easier. The strawberries are less likely to rot, too, which is common when they are exposed to wet soil on the ground. Simply follow these steps to make a basket of fruit that looks as good as it tastes.

Alpine or wild strawberries are very easy to grow and fruit all summer.

CHOOSING FRUIT FOR BASKETS

You will find many different varieties of strawberry for sale, offering an assortment of flavours and fruit sizes and shapes. The large-fruited types are divided into two groups, based on when they produce a crop. Summer-fruiting varieties produce strawberries between early and late summer, while "everbearers" or perpetual types fruit through the summer and early autumn. Alternatively, you could opt for alpine or wild strawberries, the small sweet fruits of which appear from summer to early autumn. They also grow well in part shade, unlike the larger varieties, which prefer full sun. Strawberries are usually sold from autumn to spring as bareroot plants known as runners, but you may also find them for sale in pots.

HOW TO PLANT

In spring, buy a large basket that will accommodate your strawberry plants – one with a 40cm (16in) diameter is ideal. Most come with a plastic liner but if yours does not, use an old plastic bag to line the base. Make some drainage holes in the liner to prevent the plants from becoming waterlogged. Top up the basket with homemade potting compost (see pp.96–97) and plant your berries so that the crown (where the roots meet the stems) is buried but the stems and leaves are exposed to the light. Three or four strawberry plants will fill a large basket, but you may need six or seven alpines. Firm the plants in gently and water well. Suspend your basket from a sturdy hook attached to a house wall or other structure in the garden and keep the plants well-watered.

> **TOP TIP** USE THE RUNNERS (THE SMALL PLANTS THAT DEVELOP AT THE END OF LONG STEMS) OF SUMMER-FRUITING VARIETIES TO MAKE NEW PLANTS. SIMPLY INSERT THE ROOTED ENDS INTO CONTAINERS FILLED WITH POTTING MIX. KEEP WATERED AND WHEN NEW GROWTH EMERGES A FEW MONTHS LATER, CUT THE STEM FROM THE PARENT PLANT.

Set your basket in a large empty pot to stabilize it while you plant it up.

This basket is planted with everbearer strawberries that fruit from summer to early autumn.

CARING FOR STRAWBERRIES

In the first year, you can remove some of the flowers on summer-fruiting varieties to encourage the plants to put their energies into healthy growth rather than making fruit. This practice should deliver heavier crops in subsequent years – plants are productive for up to four years. On everbearers, remove some of the flowers that appear in spring to promote a later crop in autumn. These varieties tend to fruit best in the first or second year and will

then need replacing. Alpines will fruit year after year and you do not need to take off the flowers.

As the flowers of large-fruiting types fade, apply a homemade compost or plant tea (see pp.82–83) every week or two by watering on the diluted mixture. After the plants have cropped, remove dead or dying leaves and cut back the stems to 10cm (4in) above the soil surface – just remove old foliage from everbearers. Strawberry plants are hardy and can remain outside in winter, but if the flowers start to develop before the last frosts in spring, protect your plants with fleece.

Remove some or all of the flowers of summer-bearing strawberries in the first year after planting to encourage a bumper crop the following year.

PLANTING A SACK OF POTATOES

If you have limited space for growing your own vegetables, this sack of potato plants will work perfectly, allowing you to raise a crop on a balcony or patio. You can combine homemade compost and garden soil to fill the sack, and unlike plastic growing bags, the material is biodegradable so it can be cut up and added to your compost bin after a year or two, or whenever it is no longer usable.

Growing potatoes in sacks is an easy project for children to try.

The sacks sold for storing potatoes are also perfect for growing them in.

CHOOSING VARIETIES

In winter, select your favourite potato varieties from seed suppliers' catalogues and websites, or be adventurous and try new flavours. So-called "earlies" are planted in mid-spring and produce an early summer crop, while "maincrop" varieties are planted in late spring for harvesting from midsummer. If you have space for two sacks, one of each will prolong your harvest. Whichever type you choose, place the tubers in an eggbox about six to eight weeks before you plan to plant them out and set them in a cool, light place. When the shoots that develop are about 2.5cm (1in) long, you can plant them in your sack.

Letting potato tubers develop shoots before planting is known as "chitting".

SOURCING A SACK

You can buy tightly woven hessian sacks for storing potatoes from garden centres or online and these will work equally well for growing the plants. Alternatively, you can use any strong fabric bag or sack, as long as it is at least 45cm (18in) wide and deep, or grow your crops in an old dustbin or tub with drainage holes drilled in the base. Choose the largest container you can fit into your space, which will allow you to grow more tubers for a heavier crop.

Gradually add more potting mix, covering the stems as they grow, until the sack is almost full.

FILLING THE SACK

To prevent the wet compost from rotting the bottom of the sack too quickly, line the base with a piece of recycled plastic or an old metal baking tray with a couple of drainage holes drilled into it. Then add a 15cm (6in) layer of potting mix made from your homemade compost, soil, and leafmould (see p.96). Place 2–3 tubers on top, spacing them evenly about 15cm (6in) apart. Make sure the shoots are facing upwards. Cover with another 15cm (6in) of potting mix and water well. When the shoots are about 20cm (8in) tall, apply more potting mix to cover the stems so that only the leafy tips of the plants are above the surface. Continue to add more potting mix to cover the stems until the sack is almost full. Keep the plants well watered and apply a solution of compost or plant tea (see pp.82–83), or a seaweed-based fertilizer, every week.

TOP TIP POTATO SACKS WILL BE VERY HEAVY ONCE FILLED WITH POTTING MIX, SO PLANT THEM UP ALREADY SITED IN A WARM, SUNNY SPOT.

HARVESTING YOUR CROP

Early potatoes will be ready to lift when the plants are in flower, but wait until the foliage dies back before lifting maincrop varieties. You can feel around in the compost to check that the tubers are well developed before lifting them.

To harvest your potatoes, either tip the potting mix and plants out of sacks that are intact and could be washed and used again, or cut the bags open to reveal your crop. Once you have removed the tubers, add the old plants to your compost heap. You could then refill sturdy sacks with potting mix and sow a quick crop such as lettuces or radishes that will mature before winter.

Early potato varieties will produce a crop of tasty tubers in early summer.

TRY TOMATOES

Potatoes and tomatoes are from the plant genus *Solanum* and the latter can be grown in sacks too. You can plant tomatoes in the same potting mix as potatoes, using smaller bags. Patio varieties are an ideal choice or, if you choose a cordon tomato, add a stake when planting and pinch out the stems growing between the main and side stems as soon as you spot them. Set tomatoes outside when the frosts have passed, or grow indoor varieties in a greenhouse.

Add a tall stake such as a bamboo cane to support the stems of tall cordon tomato varieties.

GROWING BEANS IN A COMPOST TRENCH

Runner and French beans benefit from soil improved with homemade compost that holds nutrients and water well. They are tender plants and should not be set outside until all risk of frost has passed in late spring, but you can sow seed in pots indoors earlier to get a head start. Beans will need a sturdy support for their long climbing stems, but once established they are otherwise very easy to grow.

Runner beans growing on a large cane pyramid will produce a crop to feed a family for many weeks in summer.

Dig a compost trench for your bean plants in a sunny, sheltered spot.

TRENCH TREASURES

Compost trenches create the perfect growing conditions for bean plants. About a month before planting in late spring, dig a trench about 30cm (12in) deep, 60cm (24in) wide, and as long as you need to space the plants you plan to grow 25cm (10in) apart. Partially fill the hole with finished or almost finished compost and mix some more into the excavated soil before replacing it. Alternatively, in autumn or late winter, follow the steps for making a trench filled with kitchen and garden waste (see pp.62–63) – this will rot down by late spring, ready for planting, and may also generate a little extra heat to boost the beans' initial growth.

CREATING A SUPPORT

Build a support for the beans over the trench. If you only have a small space you can make a circular trench and install a pyramid of tall, sturdy canes, tied at the top with strong twine. Where you plan to grow beans in rows, create a longer tent-shaped support with canes or pruned stems and secure them to another cane at the top, as shown. Sow one or two beans, or plant one young seedling, at the base of each cane when all risk of frost has passed.

To grow two rows of beans, make a tent-shaped support using canes 2.4m (8ft) long, with one at the top for stability.

Tie young stems to their cane support and they will then wind around and climb up it without help as they grow.

CARING FOR BEANS

As the beans start to grow, tie their young stems to their supports. They will then start to twine around the canes of their own accord and climb to the top unaided. Water plants well while they are establishing and especially when the flowers appear. In summer, you can also add a 5cm (2in) mulch of homemade compost around the plants after rain has fallen to help lock in the moisture. Pinch out the growing tips when the plants reach the tops of their supports.

Picking your beans regularly encourages the plant to produce more crops.

HARVESTING YOUR CROPS

Beans are tender and tastiest when picked young, so check plants as soon as you see the pods start to develop and harvest them regularly. Picking the beans will also encourage the plants to produce more flowers and pods, helping to extend the harvest time. When the temperatures start to soar in summer, water the plants more frequently to prevent crop failure.

TOP TIP CUT OFF THE BOTTOMS AND TOPS OF LARGE PLASTIC DRINKS BOTTLES AND POP THEM OVER EACH BEAN SEEDLING TO KEEP THE YOUNG PLANTS WARM AND HELP TO PROTECT THEM FROM SLUGS AND SNAILS.

PLANTING TREES AND SHRUBS

Trees and shrubs make a valuable contribution to any garden, offering height, structure, colour, and shade. They also perform an important role in reducing air pollution by absorbing large volumes of carbon dioxide, which contributes to global warming, and releasing oxygen back into the atmosphere. Your homemade compost and leafmould will help to get these plants off to a good start.

Himalayan birches (*Betula utilis*), with their gleaming white stems and airy canopies of diamond-shaped leaves, are a good choice for small gardens.

CHOOSING TREES AND SHRUBS

Before buying a tree or shrub, assess your garden conditions, including the soil type (see *pp.12–13*) and how much sun and shade it receives, to ensure that the plants you have in mind will thrive there. Also check each plant's final height and spread to make sure it will not outgrow the space allocated for it, since moving a mature tree or shrub from the wrong position is not an easy task. In a small garden, opt for a tree that has a few seasons of interest, such as spring blossom and autumn fruits or colourful leaves. Compact cherry (*Prunus*), crab apple (*Malus*), and hawthorn trees (*Crataegus*) are ideal, or opt for an evergreen such as holly (*Ilex*), which will decorate the garden with glossy leaves year-round and red berries in autumn and winter. Consider a tree's shape, too; a tall, slim specimen may work better in a small space than a shorter, broader plant. Scented shrubs, including mahonias, daphnes, sweet box (*Sarcoccoca confusa*), and *Viburnum carlesii* will also add to the sensory delights of the garden. A specialist tree and shrub nursery will be able to advise you on other good choices for your specific site and needs.

Hawthorns are compact trees with pretty spring blossom that is loved by pollinators, followed by red autumn berries.

TOP TIP POT-GROWN SHRUBS CAN BE PLANTED AT ANY TIME OF THE YEAR, BUT AVOID THE SUMMER MONTHS WHEN THE SOIL IS DRY AND PLANTS WILL NEED WATERING MORE FREQUENTLY.

Hardy shrubs such as *Viburnum carlesii*, which produces its scented flowers in spring, are best planted in autumn.

BEFORE PLANTING

Most trees and shrubs thrive in a water-retentive soil that also drains well, which are the exact conditions a mulch of home-made compost will deliver (see *also pp.90–95*). The best time to plant a bare-root tree or shrub is in the autumn; ideally, you should apply a mulch to the proposed site a year beforehand so that the worms have time to bring it down into the soil and improve its structure. If this is not possible, mix some compost with the soil you have excavated when digging the planting hole. Avoid planting when the soil is frozen, waterlogged, or bone-dry.

1

2

3

4

PLANTING A TREE OR SHRUB

1 Plant shrubs at the same level as they were growing in their pots or the soil (look for the dark soil mark on the stems of bare-root plants). Trees should be planted at the same level or slightly proud of the surface. Dig a hole to the depth of the root ball and three times as wide. Loosen the sides of the hole with a fork if the soil is compacted.

2 Tease out the roots of plants grown in pots to help them grow away more easily, and trim off any black or damaged roots from bare-root types.

3 Place the plant in the hole and use a cane to check it is at the right depth. Refill the hole with the excavated soil, and compost if using it at this stage (see opposite).

4 Use your toe to press the soil down around the stem to remove any air pockets. Water well and then apply a 5–7.5cm (2–3in) mulch of shredded mature wood chips (see also p.91 for advice on using wood chips), well-rotted compost, or one-year-old leafmould on the soil over the root ball, leaving a 10cm (4in) gap around the stem.

STAKING AND AFTERCARE

Large trees or those planted in windy sites will need staking after planting. Hammer in a stake at a 45-degree angle on the opposite side of the tree to the prevailing wind direction, making sure that about one third of its length is beneath the ground. Secure it to the stem with a tree tie and remove it only when the root ball no longer moves as you gently shake the tree stem. Water all newly planted trees and shrubs regularly during dry spells for 3–5 years after planting to ensure good root growth. Drench the area well once or twice a week so that water percolates down to the roots at lower levels, rather than giving small quantities more often, which encourages roots to grow towards the surface where the soil is drier and they will be more prone to drought stress. Mulch around your tree or shrub with your homemade products (see step 4) every year, in autumn on clay soils or in spring on lighter sandy soils.

Use a tree tie to secure the trunk to the stake and loosen it as the tree grows.

GROWING FOOD FOR WILDLIFE

Using plants to attract wildlife into your garden has many benefits for both you and the creatures that visit. At a time when scientists are recording sharp declines in the numbers of insects worldwide, a wildlife-friendly garden can help to reverse this trend by creating a sanctuary for bees and butterflies. Likewise, many bird species are under threat due to habitat loss and pesticides that kill their prey.

Wildlife borders next to a path allow you to enjoy watching the bees and butterflies your plants will attract.

GO WILD IN YOUR BORDERS

Just one border dedicated to wildlife can significantly increase the biodiversity in your garden. Choose a spot in full sun or part shade, as these locations will support the greatest number of plant species, which in turn will provide food for more types of wildlife. Also make your border as large as possible to accommodate a wide range of shrubs and flowers. If you are creating a border from a lawn, try lasagne composting (see pp.64–65) to remove the grass and improve the soil, or dig up the turf and compost it (see pp.71).

Sun-loving rockroses (*Cistus*) produce a long succession of large, pollen-rich flowers in summer, which attract bumblebees and other pollinating insects.

Cram in as many plants as possible, such as tickseed, penstemons, and bellflowers, which support many pollinating insects.

FOOD AND SHELTER

Prepare the soil and follow the planting advice for making a flowerbed (see pp.108–109), then draw up a list of the plants you want to grow. Choose shrubs for the back of the border, checking their final heights and spreads before planting to make sure that they will not shade the plants in front, where you can plant an array of pollen- and nectar-rich perennials, bulbs, and annuals. Also look at the flowering times of the plants and plan a continuous feast for beneficial insects throughout the year, since some pollinators will be active even in winter.

Birds and small mammals can also benefit when the flowers fade and form nutrient-rich seeds for them to eat.

In addition to the plants, you can include other features in your border to attract wildlife. Small piles of logs set between the shrubs will attract hibernating insects and offer shelter for frogs, toads, and other garden wildlife. The insects will also provide a nutritious snack for birds and their young. Laying twiggy prunings on the soil surface towards the back of the border will provide cover for small creatures, too, and the stems will gradually rot down to improve the soil (see p.69).

PLANT CHOICES

A = *annual*; B = *bulb*; C = *climber*;
P = *perennial*; S = *shrub*; T = *tree*

FLOWERS FOR POLLINATORS

The plants below provide pollen and nectar for a range of beneficial insects such as bees, butterflies, and hoverflies.

SPRING Ornamental onion (*Allium*) B • Cuckoo flower (*Cardamine pratensis*) P • Spring crocus (*Crocus vernus*) B • Snake's head fritillary (*Fritillaria meleagris*) B • Honeysuckle (*Lonicera periclymenum*) C • Grape hyacinth (*Muscari armeniacum*) B

SUMMER Butterfly bush (*Buddleja davidii*) S • Bellflower (*Campanula*) P • Rock rose (*Cistus*) S • Cosmos (*Cosmos bipinnatus*) A • Common foxglove (*Digitalis*) P • Cranesbill (*Geranium*) P • Sneezeweed (*Helenium*) P • English lavender (*Lavandula angustifolia*) S • Tobacco plant (*Nicotiana*) A • Common poppy (*Papaver rhoeas*) A • Penstemon (*Penstemon*) P • Sage (*Salvia*) S or P

AUTUMN AND WINTER Cornelian cherry (*Cornus mas*) S • Winter aconite (*Eranthis hyemalis*) B • Mahonia (*Mahonia × media* and *Mahonia aquifolium*) S • Coneflower (*Rudbeckia*) P • Single-flowered New England aster (*Symphyotrichum novae-angliae*) P

PLANTS FOR BIRDS

The spring shrubs and small trees shown below offer safe nesting sites for birds as well as berries for them to eat later in the year; other shrubs provide an autumn and winter store of fruits. The annuals and perennials produce nutrient-rich seeds that attract birds.

SPRING Japanese quince (*Chaenomeles speciosa*) S • Common hawthorn (*Crataegus monogyna*) T • Ivy (*Hedera helix*) C • Yew (*Taxus baccata*) T

SUMMER Tickseed (*Coreopsis verticillata*) P • Globe thistle (*Echinops ritro*) P • Sunflower (*Helianthus annuus*) A • Annual honesty (*Lunaria annua*) A

AUTUMN AND WINTER Japanese barberry (*Berberis thunbergia*) S • Mezereon (*Daphne mezereum*) S • Common holly (*Ilex aquifolium*) T • Firethorn (*Pyracantha*) S • Elder (*Sambucus nigra*) S • New England Aster (*Symphyotrichum novae-angliae*) P

Cardamine pratensis

Buddleja davidii

Cosmos bipinnatus

Cornus mas

Taxus baccata

Coreopsis verticillata

Echinops ritro

Ilex aquifolium

MAKING A BOG GARDEN FOR WILDLIFE

Your plant choices are partly determined by the soil conditions in your plot, but you can widen the range by using your homemade compost to help create an area of moist ground known as a bog garden. Plants adapted to the damp soil beside pools and streams will thrive there, creating a habitat for pollinators drawn to their flowers, as well as amphibians which will take cover beneath the leaves.

Widen your plant choices by creating an area of damp soil in the garden.

Hostas and moisture-loving primulas, irises, and many ferns thrive in boggy soil.

WHAT IS A BOG GARDEN?

An area of boggy soil will occur close to a natural pond where water breaks the banks after heavy rainfall. If you have such an area in your garden already, you can use it for a range of beautiful plants that enjoy wet soils. If you do not have a pond or you have installed one in an area of free-draining sandy soil that dries out quickly, you can still enjoy these moisture-loving plants by making a bog garden with some pond liner (see *opposite*). In a small garden, you could sink a watertight half barrel into the ground and plant it with baskets of marginals such as marsh marigolds (*Caltha palustris*) or a dwarf waterlily (*Nymphaea pygmaea*) to provide some open water for frogs and toads, then surround it with a bog garden to broaden your biodiversity further.

ESTABLISHING A BOG GARDEN

To provide a suitable site for a bog garden, choose a partly shaded spot that receives sun for about half the day from spring to early autumn. This location will help to ensure that the soil does not dry out too quickly in hot summer sun.

Make the bog garden in early spring so that your plants can establish quickly when the soil warms up, siting the sun-loving species you have chosen in the area that receives the most light during the summer months. Once the garden is established, use rainwater from a butt, or tap water if you have no other source, to top up the moisture levels during hot or windy weather.

The bog garden will also benefit from an annual mulch of homemade compost applied each spring, which will help to lock moisture into the soil by reducing evaporation from the surface. As the mulch continues to decompose it will also help to restock the soil with the nutrients bog plants need to thrive.

The pollen-rich flowers of the leopard plant (*Ligularia* 'The Rocket') will lure bees to your bog garden.

HOW TO MAKE A BOG GARDEN

YOU WILL NEED String or chalk • Spade •
Pond liner or recycled plastic sheet •
Bricks or stones • Fork • Rake • Gravel
or coarse grit • Well-rotted homemade
compost • Scissors or knife • Range
of bog plants (see *below*)

1 Mark out an area for your bog garden
using string or chalk and dig out the
soil to a depth of about 60cm (2ft).
Set the soil to one side. Place the liner
or plastic sheet in the hole and push
it into the corners. Weigh down the
edges of the liner at the top of the
hole with bricks or stones.

2 Using a fork, pierce the liner at
60–90cm (2–3ft) intervals to create
drainage holes – you want the area
to retain water but not to become
completely waterlogged.

3 To ensure that the drainage holes
do not become blocked over time,
causing the soil in your bog to stagnate,
cover the liner with a 7.5cm (3in) layer
of gravel or coarse grit.

4 Fill the bog garden with the soil you
excavated when digging the hole,
together with some well-rotted
homemade compost. Cut any visible
excess liner from around the edges.
Add a few cans of water from a water
butt and leave to drain. Plant up with
bog plants and add a 5cm (2in)
compost mulch.

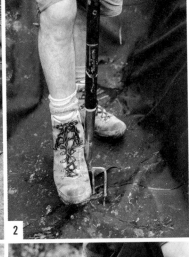

NEED TO KNOW
• Bog plants like moist soil but they
do require some drainage and air
around their roots, unlike aquatic
plants, the roots of which are
submerged beneath the water.
• If your bog garden has an area
of compacted soil that is always
waterlogged, break up the hard
pan on the surface with a fork
and add a 5–7.5cm (2–3in) mulch
of compost to improve the soil
structure and increase drainage.

PLANTS FOR WILDLIFE-FRIENDLY BOG GARDENS
Marsh marigold (*Caltha palustris*) • Umbrella plant (*Darmera peltata*) •
Gravel root (*Eupatorium purpureum*) • Meadowsweet (*Filipendula
purpurea* and *F. ulmaria*) • Water avens (*Geum rivale*) • Moisture-loving
irises (*Iris ensata* or *I. sibirica*) • Leopard plant (*Ligularia* 'The Rocket') •
Gooseneck loosestrife (*Lysimachia clethroides*) • Purple loosestrife
(*Lythrum salicaria*) • Hostas (*Hosta*) • Bee's primrose (*Primula beesiana*) •
Candelabra primula (*Primula japonica*) • Ornamental rhubarb (*Rheum
palmatum*) • Burnet (*Sanguisorba*)

TOP TIP DO NOT STOCK YOUR BOG GARDEN WITH INVASIVE PLANTS SUCH AS
GIANT RHUBARB (*GUNNERA MANICATA* OR *GUNNERA TINCTORIA*), SKUNK CABBAGE
(*LYSICHITON AMERICANUS*), OR GIANT BUTTERBUR (*PETASITES JAPONICUS*).

MAKING A MODERN ROSE GARDEN

Roses thrive in the moist, well-structured soil homemade compost helps to deliver, and you can keep them blooming beautifully year after year with annual mulching. Use disease-resistant modern cultivars or plant a species rose, which may only flower once a year but most also produce large hips after the blooms have faded. Then encircle your roses with annuals and perennials for a long-lasting display.

The stems of *Rosa* 'Louise Odier' have been threaded through a rustic woven twig support to create a colourful focal point in a mixed border.

CHOOSING ROSES

When selecting roses, look for disease-resistance and repeat-flowering shrub varieties, which will bloom throughout summer and early autumn if you remove the faded flowers regularly. Also look for those with fragrant flowers that will greet you with their sweet perfume as you enter the garden. Good choices include the white 'Winchester Cathedral', apricot 'Buff Beauty', and yellow 'Charlotte', although specialist rose breeders will have hundreds to choose from in a wide range of colours on their websites. Species roses such as *Rosa moyesii* and *R. glauca* offer an alternative. Most have a more relaxed habit than named roses but they too are disease-resistant and their colourful hips are an added bonus.

> **TOP TIP** WHEN THE BLOOMS OF REPEAT-FLOWERING ROSES FADE, CUT THEM OFF WITH SHARP SECATEURS. "DEADHEADING" IN THIS WAY WILL STIMULATE THE PLANT TO MAKE MORE BLOOMS AND KEEP IT LOOKING NEAT.

The beautiful rose 'Winchester Cathedral' is teamed with complementary perennials in this elegant white scheme.

The **pink roses** 'Silas Marner' and 'Ballerina' make beautiful partners for geraniums, *Alchemilla mollis, Erigeron karvinskianus*, loosestrife (*Lythrum*), and lavender.

PERFECT PARTNERS

Lavender and hardy geraniums such as the blue ROZANNE are often combined with roses, and look especially beautiful if paired with pink cultivars. When choosing other perennial or annual partners, check that they will not grow so tall that they cast shade on your rose and select those that have contrasting shapes and colours. For example, the spiked flowerheads of perennials such as veronicas, salvias, and loosestrife (*Lythrum*) work well with the rounded shape of most rose bushes, while *Erigeron* daisies and the frothy lime-green blooms of *Alchemilla mollis* will make a pretty skirt around their prickly stems.

Plant a shrub rose with its graft union below the surface and add a mulch of homemade compost around the stems.

PLANTING ROSES

Choose a site in full sun for the best rose display and create a new bed in autumn or spring as described for making a flowerbed (see pp.108–109). Roses appreciate a rich soil, so incorporate a bucketful of homemade compost into the soil where you plan to plant them. Then dig a hole a little deeper and twice the diameter of the container in which you bought the rose. Place the rose in its container into the hole and, using a bamboo cane, check that the graft union (the swelling at the base of the stems) will be below the surface when the rose is planted. Wearing gloves, tip the rose out of its pot and place it in the hole, then backfill with the compost-enriched soil and firm it down around the plant.

Water in the rose thoroughly before applying a 5cm (2in) layer of homemade compost, making sure that it does not touch the stems. Keep the rose well-watered during the first growing season and reapply the mulch each year, in autumn on clay soils or in spring if you have sandy soil.

GROWING FLOWERS
FOR CUTTING

One of the joys of gardening is growing your own cut flowers
to decorate your home. Sowing annuals, planting bulbs,
and filling your borders with perennials and shrubs in soils
improved with homemade compost will produce a long
season of fresh flowers for picking. It will reduce your carbon
footprint, too, as you'll avoid buying shop-bought flowers
that are flown in from countries around the world.

Rose flowers and buds with sprays
of *Astrantia* stems make a beautiful
homegrown summer bouquet.

Snowdrops under a deciduous tree will provide fresh blooms in late winter.

TOP TIP IN MILD AREAS YOU CAN USE A 10CM (4IN) LAYER OF WELL-ROTTED COMPOST
OR LEAFMOULD TO COVER SLIGHTLY TENDER CUT-FLOWER PLANTS SUCH AS DAHLIAS
TO PROTECT THEM OVER WINTER. IN COLD GARDENS, DIG UP THE TUBERS IN AUTUMN
AFTER THE FIRST FROST HAS BLACKENED THE LEAVES AND STORE THEM INDOORS.

YEAR-ROUND DISPLAYS

For fresh indoor displays all year round,
plan a bed that will produce a succession
of flowers, seedheads, and foliage plants,
starting in early spring with snowdrops
and daffodils, and finishing the year with
rose hips and berries from holly and ivy.
Plant spring bulbs outside in autumn,
and sow some sweet peas (*Lathyrus
odoratus*) in deep pots of homemade
seed compost (see p.96) at the same
time. Overwinter the seedlings in an
unheated greenhouse, cold frame, or
cool room indoors before planting
them in the garden the following spring.

In spring, sow annuals such as cosmos,
sunflowers, and zinnias for picking later
in summer. Start off dahlia tubers in
containers indoors and repot the
young plants outside after the frosts
have passed in early summer. Other
summer bulbs can be planted in late
spring directly in the garden.

You can also cut perennial plants,
including alstroemerias, sea holly
(*Eryngium*), rudbeckias, ferns, and
ornamental grasses, which you can
plant in your borders in spring to
decorate your home throughout
summer and early autumn. Repeat-
flowering roses (see pp.126–127) will
also produce a succession of blooms.

Grow flowers such as chrysanthemums on an allotment in rows like a vegetable crop or at home in groups in a flowerbed.

PLANTING A BED FOR CUT FLOWERS

Prepare the ground as described for a flowerbed (see pp.108–109) in a sunny, sheltered spot with moist but free-draining soil – mulching the bed a year before planting and annually thereafter will help to produce the ideal conditions (see pp.90–95).

You can either plant your flowers in rows like a vegetable crop or in large groups of each type of plant, if you want to cut a few blooms every week or two without creating a hole in your garden display. Many annuals used for cutting do not like rich soil and may develop more leaves than blooms if nutrients levels are too high. This is rarely a problem on sandy, free-draining soils, but if you have heavy clay, a mulch of homemade compost applied the autumn before you plant your annuals will help to improve the drainage, which these plants will prefer.

CHOOSING FLOWERS

The flowers listed below make beautiful indoor displays. Water your plants well the night before picking, which plumps up the stems and prolongs the life of the flowers when they are in a vase. Harvest your flowers first thing in the morning, cutting them just above a leaf or node (bump) on the stem. Then strip the lower leaves from the stems and plunge them up to their necks in a bucket of very cold water. Leave them there for 24 hours before arranging them.

A = annual; B = bulbs; Bi = biennial; P = perennial

Allium B • Alstroemeria P • Snapdragon (Antirrhinum) A • Astrantia P • Chrysanthemum P • Spider flower (Cleome) A • Cosmos A • Dahlia B • Sweet william (Dianthus barbatus) Bi • Foxglove (Digitalis) Bi • Sea holly (Eryngium) P • Sunflower (Helianthus annuus) A • Sweet pea (Lathyrus odoratus) A • Daffodil (Narcissus) B • Peony (Paeonia) P • Cut-leaved coneflower (Rudbeckia laciniata) P • Tulip (Tulipa) B • Zinnia A

Cut your fresh flowers early in the morning after watering the plants the night before to plump up the stems.

Tie flowers into small bunches and hang them up in an airy room to dry.

DRYING FLOWERS

You can prolong homegrown flower displays by drying suitable blooms too. Statice (Limonium), everlasting flowers (Xerochrysum), and love-in-a-mist (Nigella) are good choices, but these all like poor, free-draining soils, so if you garden on clay, it may be best to grow them in raised beds filled with a mixture of imported topsoil and horticultural grit. Even on free-draining sandy soils, do not be tempted to use your compost on the beds where you are growing these annuals, as it may increase the fertility and reduce flowering.

Cut the stems on a dry day, just before the flowers are fully open, and tie a few stems together with string. Attach the bunches to string or a cane suspended across a cool, airy, dark room, and leave for a couple of weeks until the flowers feel crisp and dry.

FLOWERS FOR DRYING Achillea • Globe thistle (Echinops) • Lavender (Lavandula) • Statice (Limonium) • Love-in-a-mist (Nigella damascena) • Everlasting flowers (Xerochrysum)

REPOTTING SHRUBS

Large woody plants can remain in their pots for some years, but they will eventually outgrow their living quarters and need repotting. When planting a shrub, choose a container that either has straight sides or is wider at the top than the bottom. This will ensure that the rootball is easy to remove when the time comes to transfer the plant to a larger pot – you may have to break vessels that have smaller necks than bases to extract the roots.

Plant shrubs in containers with a wider top than the base, such as this half-barrel, to make repotting easier.

TIME TO MOVE

Shrubs and small trees in decorative containers make beautiful focal points on a patio or balcony, but after a few years they may start to show signs of poor growth. This is often because the roots have filled the pot and become congested, which means that they will not be able to take up water or nutrients easily. If this is the case, the top of the potting mix in your container will be a solid mat of roots and the leaves may turn yellow and fall off. The plant's susceptibility to pests and diseases can increase too.

Yellow leaves and poor growth are signs that a shrub may have outgrown its pot.

Hebes require a gritty potting mix to ensure there is good drainage around the plant's roots.

CHOOSING A POTTING MIX

Before you move your shrub, make up an appropriate potting mix for its new container, which should be one or two sizes larger than the original pot. Most shrubs will thrive in a 50:50 mix of homemade compost and garden soil, but those that like free-draining conditions such as lavender and bay trees (*Laurus nobilis*) will prefer a grittier mix of one part soil, one part homemade compost or leafmould, and one part horticultural sand or grit. Make up enough to half-fill the new pot you have chosen, which should fill it once the plant is added.

REPLANTING SHRUBS

Give your plants a long drink before repotting, and leave the water to percolate down into the root ball – this may take a while when the roots are congested. Slide an old bread knife around the edge of the root ball to loosen it from the sides and tip the pot on its side on to a soft surface such as a lawn, so that you do not scratch the container. You will probably need someone to hold the pot while you slide the plant out.

Add a layer of your potting mix to the bottom of the new container, checking that once the shrub is planted the base

of its stem will be about 5cm (2in) below the rim, which will allow sufficient space for water to collect before it seeps into the soil. Use a hose to wash off some of the old compost from the root ball, then carefully tease out the roots, which will be tightly encircling the central ball. Trim off any that look black or diseased, then place the plant in the container and fill in around it with fresh potting mix. Shake the shrub gently to settle the potting mix around the roots. After watering, add a 2.5cm (1in) mulch of homemade compost or leafmould over the surface of the potting mix, leaving a gap around the shrub's stems.

NEED TO KNOW

- Water your plant regularly. Give it plenty of water each time rather than delivering it in short bursts, so that it penetrates down to the roots instead of encouraging them up to the surface where they will dry out.
- Keep your repotted shrub out of direct sunshine and drying winds for a few weeks until you see new leaves or stems start to grow.
- Top up the mulch of homemade potting compost or leafmould each year in spring.

Take care to protect your back by bending your knees and asking a friend to hold the pot before pulling the plant out.

Wash off some of the compost around the roots and then gently tease out those encircling the root ball with your fingers.

Use homemade potting mix to fill in around the roots of the replanted shrub before adding a compost mulch on top.

KEEPING PLANTS COMPACT

Instead of repotting, you can trim the roots of your shrub and replace it in its original container. This method will help to keep large shrubs more compact and is good option if you do not have space for a larger pot. Follow the advice for repotting above, but once you have extracted the plant

from its container use a clean, sharp pair of secateurs to remove up to a third of the roots. Cut through some of the thicker roots, which stabilize the plant, but retain as many of the fine roots as possible – these smaller roots draw up the most water and nutrients. Then plant up the root-trimmed shrub as described above.

Trim the roots with sharp secateurs to keep your shrub compact.

PLANTING SPRING BULBS

Spring bulbs light up the garden as soon as temperatures start to rise, providing a dazzling display of flower colours, textures, shapes, and sizes to welcome in the new season. Plant them in autumn to bloom the following year and many will then return year after year with little aftercare, apart from a mulch of homemade compost. You can add bulbs to containers, too, using your own materials to pot them up.

Plant your spring bulbs in autumn in soil improved with homemade compost.

CHOOSING SPRING BULBS

There are bulbs for every garden and they come in all colours of the rainbow, from sunny yellow daffodils to smouldering dark red tulips and bright blue grape hyacinths (*Muscari*). You may also want to try a few lesser-known bulbs such as the elegant white spring and summer snowflakes (*Leucojum*) and dainty Sicilian honey garlic (*Nectaroscordum siculum*), which are just as easy as daffodils to grow and will reappear every spring after planting. Make a list of your favourites and include flowers for each month to create a continuous display, with late tulips and alliums delivering a spectacular finale as the seasons turn.

Allium cernuum produces pink pendent flowers.

Allium 'Gladiator' adds impact when grown in groups.

Narcissus 'Canaliculatus' is ideal for growing in containers.

Tulipa 'Artist' is a striking orange and green variety.

Tulipa 'Dreamland' bears white-edged pink flowers.

Tulipa 'Purissima' adds an elegant note to a border.

Nectaroscordum siculum produces unusual flowers.

Muscari are available in many different shades of blue.

PLANTING IN BEDS

Most bulbs enjoy free-draining soil, so if you have heavy clay, improve it with a mulch of homemade compost in autumn and reapply it every year at the same time. If you are just starting out and your soil does not drain well, choose daffodils (*Narcissus*) and camassias, which will cope better than most with wetter conditions. Spring bulbs such as tulips and daffodils will also benefit from a compost mulch laid over free-draining soils in early spring. Mulching lighter soils will prevent vital plant nutrients from being washed away, which will encourage the bulbs to flower year after year.

Plant spring bulbs in autumn in full sun or part shade and remember that areas beneath trees that receive little sun in summer will probably have enough light to promote flowering in spring, before the canopies unfurl. Most bulbs should be planted beneath the soil at 2–3 times their own depth; for example, a daffodil bulb measuring 5cm (2in) would be planted 10–15cm (4–6in) deep. If you have clay soil, plant tulips a little deeper, about 20cm (8in) below the surface, and on a layer of grit, which encourages the bulbs to bloom for more than one year; ask a reputable supplier for varieties most likely to repeat flower. Plant all bulbs with the pointed end up.

Elegant camassias are the perfect choice for heavier clay soils.

Plant tulip bulbs in a pot quite close together but not touching.

Layer tulip, daffodil, and grape hyacinth bulbs in one large pot for a mixed display.

POTTING UP BULBS

Tulips, daffodils, and grape hyacinths are good choices for container displays, while crocuses, dwarf irises, and species tulips will create a splash of colour in alpine troughs. Plant your bulbs in autumn, in an equal mix of homemade compost, garden soil, and leafmould – add some horticultural grit or sand when planting tulips or an alpine trough. You can also layer the bulbs in a large pot, planting tulips on about 10cm (4in) of potting mix at the bottom, followed

by a 5cm (2in) layer of potting mix and some daffodils on top of this. Add more potting mix and finally plant grape hyacinths at the top, so that they are about 5cm (2in) below the surface. Either choose varieties that all flower at the same time, or opt for a progression of blooms if you prefer. Make sure your containers have drainage holes and set them on pot feet to prevent the soil mix from becoming waterlogged. Place the pots in a sheltered spot overwinter and bring them into a sunny or partly shaded area when the shoots appear in spring.

ANNUAL CARE

After your bulbs have bloomed, nip out the dying flowers with your fingers or cut them off with secateurs. This will prevent the plants from putting their energies into making seed rather than increasing the bulb size, from which a new flower will appear the following year. Leave the foliage to die down naturally as this also helps the plant to store nutrients and energy in the bulb, ready for its next outing. You can use the space left after the bulbs have finished to plant summer bedding.

Remove the flowerheads of daffodils and other bulbs as they begin to fade to prevent them from making seeds.

POTTING UP HOUSEPLANTS

Houseplants will need repotting if they outgrow their original pots, or if their containers lack drainage holes, which can lead to waterlogged soil and root rot. Replanting in a slightly larger pot with good drainage will allow your plants to develop new healthy growth and ensure they do not drown. Use your homemade compost to create a potting mix suitable for your particular houseplants.

Plant leafy tropical plants such as umbrella trees (*Schefflera*) in a mix of soil, homemade compost and sand.

SIGNS OF STRESS

Your houseplant will need repotting if the leaves turn yellow and fall off more frequently than usual, or it is showing other signs of poor growth, such as failing to flower. Roots growing through the drainage holes at the bottom of the pot and tightly encircling the root ball can also stunt growth. A plant suffering this type of stress is described as being "root bound" or "pot bound", and it should be transferred into a larger container filled with fresh potting mix.

Succulents will thrive in an equal mix of garden soil, homemade compost, and horticultural sand.

Roots growing out of the bottom of a plant's container is one of the signs that it needs repotting.

ALL MIXED UP

You can make your own potting mixes for houseplants, just as you can for outdoor containers (see pp.96–97), using a range of homemade materials. Compost and soil mixes will be perfect for repotting, but remember that not all houseplants like the same growing medium. Most palms prefer a mix of 3 parts soil-based compost made from equal quantities of garden soil and homemade compost (or soil made with bokashi – see p.79), together with 1 part horticultural sand.

Leafy houseplants from tropical regions, such as Chinese evergreens (*Aglaonema commutatum*), peacock plants (*Goeppertia makoyana*), and umbrella trees (*Schefflera*) will thrive in an equal mix of garden soil, homemade compost, and horticultural sand or perlite, which resembles the conditions in their native lands. The same combination will support succulents, such as aloes, agaves, and houseleeks (*Sempervivum*), but if you are growing cacti, make up a more free-draining mix of 3 parts soil-based compost as described above, 1 part sand, and 1 part perlite.

HOW TO REPOT YOUR HOUSEPLANTS

YOU WILL NEED A pot one size larger than the original, with drainage holes at the bottom • Potting mix to suit the plant • Decorative waterproof container (optional) • Watering can fitted with a rose head

1 Check that the new pot you have chosen is wide and deep enough to fit your plant's root ball comfortably, with some space around the edges and at the top for watering. Do not be tempted to plant into a pot much bigger than the root ball, as most plants prefer a snug fit. Water the plant about half an hour before tipping it out of its original pot.

2 Check that the potting mix you make up is suitable for your plant (see *opposite*), and then add a layer to the bottom of the new pot. If the roots are tightly congested, gently tease out those around the edge with your fingers. Then place the plant on the compost, checking that the top of the root ball will be 1cm (½in) or more below the rim of the pot when it is planted.

3 Fill in around the plant's roots with more compost, pressing it down gently to remove any air gaps. Make sure that the plant stems (and aerial roots if it has any) are not buried. The plant should be at the same depth as it was in its original pot.

4 Water the plant well so that all the compost is wet through. Tip away any excess water in the saucer under the pot. If you are using two pots, planting in one with drainage holes and putting that into an outer decorative waterproof container, tip away any water that has collected in the bottom of the outer pot to prevent waterlogging.

ANNUAL TOP-UP

Large houseplants benefit from an annual mulch of homemade compost, which will help to keep moisture locked into the potting mix and is especially effective in warm, centrally heated homes. In spring, water the plant well and then apply a 2.5cm (1in) layer of compost or leafmould over the surface, leaving a small gap around the woody stems of plants such as umbrella trees, weeping figs (*Ficus benjamina*), and rubber plants (*Ficus elastica*). The

Apply a mulch of compost to potted houseplants to help lock in moisture.

compost will slowly decompose further and the nutrients that are released will wash down to the roots as you water the plant.

GLOSSARY

This glossary offers brief explanations of the terms used in this book that relate to compost and composting methods, as well as types of plants, insects, and animals.

Actinomycetes
A form of bacteria that look like fungi and digest woody material in the compost heap or bin.

Aerobic digestion
The process of decomposition carried out by minibeasts and microorganisms that require oxygen to breathe.

Anaerobic digestion
The process of decomposition carried out by microorganisms that operate without oxygen in airless conditions, which can occur in waterlogged compost. By-products include the gases hydrogen sulphide and methane.

Annual
Plants that germinate, produce green growth, flower, set seed, and die within one year.

Biennial
Plants that germinate and produce leaves in the first year, then flower and set seed in the second year.

Biodiversity
The variety of living organisms, including microorganisms, animals, insects, fish, and plants, in a given environment or habitat. It refers to diversity within species and between species.

Bokashi composting
An anaerobic process that pickles food waste, after which it can be composted outside in a conventional bin.

Brandlings
Another term for red or tiger worms, which are used to make compost in a wormery (see pp.74–77).

Bulbs
The collective term for all plants that form underground storage organs, including bulbs, tubers, corms, and rhizomes.

Carbon:nitrogen ratio
Also known as the C:N ratio, this is the proportion of carbon to nitrogen in materials that can be added to a compost bin or heap (see p.29).

Cool composting
The process of gradual decomposition of organic matter in a heap or bin that never reaches the high temperatures in a hot compost bin (see pp.56–57).

Decomposers
The minibeasts, bacteria, fungi, and other microorganisms that decompose organic matter in a compost bin or heap (see pp.22–25).

Grassboarding
The method of sandwiching cardboard and paper between grass clippings to make compost (see p.71).

Green manure
Plants grown to protect the soil from erosion and weed growth and supply nutrients when they are dug in and break down. Nitrogen-fixing green manure plants, such as legumes, boost this key plant nutrient when they rot down in the soil (see pp.72–73).

Greenhouse gases
Air pollutants, including carbon dioxide and methane, that contribute to the warming of the Earth's atmosphere.

Hardening off
The process of acclimatizing seedlings and young plants grown indoors to the lower temperatures outdoors before they are planted in the garden.

High-fibre composting
Combines cardboard and paper products with food and garden waste materials to form compost (see pp. 60–61).

Hot composting
Also known as "traditional composting", this decomposition method makes compost very quickly by combining large quantities of brown and green organic waste that heat up to temperatures of 60–70°C (140–158°F) (see pp.54–55).

The Hugelkultur method
A method of composting woody waste by burying it in trenches along with green waste to decompose in situ (see p.69).

Humus
The carbon-rich, spongy, black-brown material that is left after decomposers have extracted all the nutrients from the organic matter in compost. Humus

is essential to the creation of good soil structure (see p.11).

Invertebrates
Creatures without a backbone, such as worms, slugs, snails, and insects.

Lasagne composting
Layering cardboard or paper with kitchen and garden waste to form compost on top of the soil (see pp.64–65) rather than in a heap or bin.

Leafmould
Decomposed leaves collected in autumn or other times, often used as mulch or in seed composts (see pp.66–67).

Lignin
The material that forms the cell walls of many woody plants, making them rigid. It is decomposed slowly by fungi and actinomycetes.

Loam
Soil with almost equal proportions of sand and clay particles that make it ideal for plant growth.

Mesophilic
Describes bacteria and other microorganisms that operate in temperatures below 45°C (113°F).

Microorganisms/Microbes
The collective term for bacteria, fungi, and other microscopic decomposers.

Mulch
A layer of organic or inorganic material such as compost and gravel, used to protect the soil surface from weed growth and evaporation. Organic mulches also rot down to improve the soil structure and deliver nutrients to plant roots.

Mycorrhizae
Fungi that grow within or around the roots of a plant in a symbiotic relationship where they provide nutrients to the plant in exchange for carbon received from the plant.

NPK value
The ratio of the key plant nutrients nitrogen (N), phosphorus (P), and potassium (K) found in fertilizer and potting mediums.

Perennial
A plant that lives for more than two years; the top growth of most, but not all, perennials dies down in winter and new growth reappears each spring.

pH value
The measurement of acidity, alkalinity, or neutrality of a soil or compost, which determines the types of plants that will thrive in it (see p.13).

Photosynthesis
The process by which plants use sunlight, carbon dioxide, and water to produce food to sustain their growth.

Pricking out
The process of replanting congested seedlings in their own pots or modules, or spacing them out further in trays of fresh compost.

Sheet composting
Another term for lasagne composting (see left).

Soil structure
The way in which individual particles of sand, silt, and clay are assembled to form larger particles (aggregates) in a soil, which affects its drainage capacity and its nutrient content.

Soil texture
The relative percentage of sand, silt, and clay within a soil which, unlike soil structure, cannot be changed by applying compost or other types of soil amendments.

Symbiosis
The interaction between two different organisms living in close physical proximity with one another, usually to the advantage of both; for example, mycorrhizal fungi and plant roots have a symbiotic relationship.

Thermophilic
Describes bacteria and other microorganisms that operate in temperatures of 50–70°C (122–158°F) in a hot compost bin.

Tiger worms
Another term for brandlings or red worms that are used to make compost in a wormery.

Trench composting
The method of digging a trench or hole in the ground and filling it with kitchen and garden waste to decompose in situ (see pp.62–63).

RESOURCES

The companies and organizations below offer advice and products for the home gardener. Also check your local authority's website for offers on compost bins at discount prices.

INFORMATION & ADVICE

Centre for Alternative Technology (CAT)
This charity devised the high-fibre composting method and offers advice on reducing waste in the garden to create a zero-carbon world.
www.cat.org.uk

Charles Dowding
A leading proponent of the no-dig method of gardening, who explains how to use composts for mulching soils.
https://charlesdowding.co.uk

Eden Project
Resources and courses on plants and plant care from the experts at the Eden Project charity in Cornwall, UK.
www.edenproject.com/learn

Friends of the Earth
A campaigning group that offers advice on gardening organically, creating your own composts, and reducing waste.
https://friendsoftheearth.uk

Garden Organic
Provides advice and courses on home composting and gardening organically.
https://gardenorganic.org.uk

Green Venture
Educational not-for-profit organization that provides information on composting and eco-friendly gardening.
https://greenventure.ca

The National Allotment Society
Advice on planning and growing crops on allotments.
www.nsalg.org.uk

Natural Environment Research Council
Funds independent environmental science, training, and innovation; add "compost" or "soils" to the search engine for the latest research articles.
https://nerc.ukri.org

Permaculture Society
Online resources and lectures on gardening organically and sustainably.
www.permaculture.org.uk

Royal Horticultural Society
For advice on all aspects of composting, plants, planting techniques, and garden care.
www.rhs.org.uk

Soil Association
This charity offers advice on home composting and protecting soils.
www.soilassociation.org

Sustainability Guide
Advice on sustainable living, including home composting and waste reduction in the garden.
www.sustainabilityguide.co.uk

Which? Gardening
Tests and reviews the best compost bins and related products on the market in the UK.
www.which.co.uk

WRAP (Waste and Resources Action Programme)
This charity promotes ways of reducing food waste and pollution levels.
www.wrap.org.uk

The Wildlife Trusts
Advice on gardening for insect pollinators and other forms of wildlife.
www.wildlifetrusts.org

The Woodland Trust
For advice on choosing and planting trees, and conservation of forests and woodlands.
www.woodlandtrust.org.uk

COMPOST BIN SUPPLIERS

gm8group
Offers a wide range of sustainable garden products including compost bins and wormeries.
www.gm8group.com

Green Johanna
Advice and a free factsheet on using a Green Johanna compost bin.
www.gronajohanna.se/wp-content/uploads/Green_Johanna_Handbook.pdf

Harrod Horticultural
Offers an exclusive range of compost bins and related equipment made in the UK.
www.harrodhorticultural.com

The Organic Gardening Catalogue
A wide selection of compost bins, wormeries, and other organic gardening products.
www.organiccatalogue.com

Original Organics
Suppliers of compost bins, wormeries, and bokashi bins.
www.originalorganics.co.uk

Wiggly Wigglers
Stylish wormeries for the home or garden, plus comprehensive advice on caring for your worms.
www.wigglywigglers.co.uk

Wormery
A wide range of wormeries and information on caring for worms.
www.wormery.co.uk

BIBLIOGRAPHY

pp.12–13 British Society of Soil Science, www.soils.org.uk

pp.14–15 The Woodland Trust: Woodwise leaflet, downloadable from www.woodlandtrust.org.uk

p.16 UK Statistics on Waste, 2020; www.gov.uk/government/statistics/uk-waste-data Facts and Figures about Materials, Waste and Recycling, www.epa.gov

p.90 WRAP: Using quality compost to benefit crops, www.wrap.org.uk

p.91 Scharenbroch, B, and Watson, G.W: 'Wood chips and compost improve soil quality and increase growth of *Acer rubrum* and *Betula nigra* in compacted urban soil', *Aboriculture & Urban Forestry*, November 2014, 40(6):319–331

INDEX

Author Zia Allaway

AUTHOR ACKNOWLEDGMENTS

Many thanks to Marek Walisiewicz at Cobalt id for commissioning me to write this book and to Paul Reid for his inspirational designs. Thanks also to editor Diana Vowles, and Amy Slack and Ruth O'Rourke at Dorling Kindersley for helping to make this fascinating subject accessible to all.

PUBLISHER ACKNOWLEDGMENTS

DK would like to thank Oreolu Grillo and Sophie State for early spread development for the series, Margaret McCormack for indexing, and Paul Reid, Marek Walisiewicz, and the Cobalt team for their hard work in putting this book together.

PICTURE CREDITS

The publisher would like to thank the following for their kind permission to reproduce their photographs:

Alamy Stock Photo: Soil Paparazzi 2c; Jim Holden 16cl; Thomas Smith 17tl; Rob Walls 21cl; H Lansdown 22bl; Science Photo Library 24tr; Gabor Havasi 25c; Olga Miltsova 26cl; Deborah Vernon 30tr; Stephen Dwyer 30cl; Oleksandr Rupeta 30br; Domen Pal 32cl; imageBROKER 34c; HERA FOOD 34cr; Nigel Cattlin 39cb2; Naturepix 39cb3; Nigel Cattlin 39cb5; Nigel Cattlin 39br; Richard Cooper 42bl; Ket Sang Tai 43tr; Global Warming Images 45br; Paul Weston 46tr; Annie Eagle 52cl; Jurate Buiviene 53tr; Alexandra 54c; Jurate Buiviene 56tr; Art Directors & TRIP 56cl; Simon Kadula 56br; Daisy-Daisy 58bl; Botany vision 58bc; Graham Corney 60tr; Panther Media GmbH 61bc; Deborah Vernon 62bl; Keith Morris 63c; Deborah Vernon 66cr; Photo-Loci 67ca; Manor Photography 70tr; Ian Wood 70bl; blickwinkel 74br; Deborah Vernon 75tl; Rachel Husband 76cr; keith burdett 86bl; Joe Blossom 87c; David Tipling Photo Library 91br; Galinast 95cl; Ken Gillespie Photography 98bl; Mim Friday 101tl; Panther Media GmbH 102c; fotoshoot 103c; JuNi Art 116cl; Tim Gainey 117tl; Lena Ason 139r.

Dorling Kindersley: 123RF.com / Vaclav Volrab 22bc; Alan Buckingham 39ca2, 39ca3,39ca4; Brian North / RHS Chelsea Flower Show 69tr, 113tr; Brian North / RHS Hampton Court Flower Show 112cr, 112c; 120tr; Brian North 100tr; 64br, 64cl, 65bc, 65br, 65c, 65cr, 65tc 65tr, 78bl, 78cr, 78tr, 79tr, 80br, 80tr, 81bc, 81br, 81c, 81cr, 81tc, 81tr, 96b, 97bl, 97br, 97tc; Dreamstime.com / Airborne77 31t; Dreamstime.com / Hdsidesign 34bl; Dreamstime.com / Photographyfirm 86bc; Dreamstime.com / Roman Kutsekon 28bl; Dreamstime.com / Stevieuk 15bl; Dreamstime.com / Subbotina 37bl; John Glover / Royal Botanic Gardens, Kew 132c3; Kim Taylor 17br; Mark Winwood / Ball Colegrave 109b2, 123c3; Mark Winwood / Marle Place Gardens and Gallery 123c4; Mark Winwood / RHS Chelsea Flower Show 123c2; Mark Winwood / RHS Wisley 109b1, 109b3, 109b4, 128bl, 132b4, 133tr; Mark Winwood 125c, 125cr, 125tc, 130cr; Peter Anderson / RHS Chelsea Flower Show 113bc, 106tr, 107br, 64tr, 122bl, 122tr; Peter Anderson / RHS Hampton Court Flower Show 13bl, 35l; Peter Anderson 60br, 108bl, 108tr, 124cl, 124tr, 126tr, 127t, RHS Tatton Park 123b2.

Getty Images: OceanProd 46br; Katrin Ray Shumakov 95bc.

Illustrations by Cobalt id.

All other images © Dorling Kindersley

Produced for DK by
COBALT ID
www.cobaltid.co.uk

Managing Editor Marek Walisiewicz
Editor Diana Vowles
Managing Art Editor Paul Reid
Art Editor Darren Bland

DK LONDON

Project Editor Amy Slack
Managing Editor Ruth O'Rourke
Managing Art Editor Christine Keilty
Production Editor David Almond
Production Controller Stephanie McConnell
Senior Jacket Designer Nicola Powling
Jacket Co-ordinator Lucy Philpott
Consultant Gardening Publisher Chris Young
Art Director Maxine Pedliham
Publishing Directors Mary-Clare Jerram, Katie Cowa

First published in Great Britain in 2021 by
Dorling Kindersley Limited
DK, One Embassy Gardens, 8 Viaduct Gardens,
London, SW11 7BW

The authorised representative in the EEA is
Dorling Kindersley Verlag GmbH.
Arnulfstr. 124, 80636 Munich, Germany

Copyright © 2021 Dorling Kindersley Limited
A Penguin Random House Company
10 9 8 7 6 5 4 3 2 1
001–321111–Mar/2021

A CIP catalogue record for this book
is available from the British Library.
ISBN: 978-0-2414-6019-1

Printed and bound in China

For the curious
www.dk.com

MIX
Paper from
responsible sources
FSC™ C018179